Commentary on Practices of a Bodhisattva

by Tenzin Gyatso
His Holiness the XIV Dalai Lama

Translated by
Acharya Nyima Tsering

Edited by
Vyvyan Cayley and Mike Gilmore

LIBRARY OF TIBETAN WORKS AND ARCHIVES

© 1995: Library of Tibetan Works & Archives Dharamsala, India.

First Print 1995
This edition 2004

ALL RIGHTS RESERVED

No part of this publication may be reproduced, stored in retrieval system, or transmitted in any form or by any means, electronic, mechanical, photo-copying, recording or otherwise, without the prior permission of the copyright publisher.

ISBN: 81-85102-97-X

Published by the Library of Tibetan Works & Archives, Dharamsala, H.P. 176215, India and printed at Indraprastha Press (CBT), 4 Bahadur Shah Zafar Marg, New Delhi 110002.

Dedication

Dedicated to the commemoration of the sixtieth birth anniversary of our peerless Lord and Protector, His Holiness the XIV Dalai Lama. May all His wishes be effortlessly fulfilled and may all His deeds become ever more glorious. May He live a long life free from obstructions.

Contents

Publisher's Note	vii
Translator's Note	ix
1. Day One	1
2. Day Two	31
3. Day Three	61
Conclusion	105
Notes	109

Publisher's Note

Thirty Seven Practices of a Bodhisattva, composed by Ngulchu Gyalsas Thogmed Zangpo, is included in the Mind Training text and may also be explained in the context of the Lam Rim tradition. It is one of the most popular texts in the development of Tibetan thought and literature and has been expounded by His Holiness the Dalai Lama on a number of occasions during Dharma teachings.

This discourse presented by His Holiness the Dalai Lama is one of the most practical. Employing a style of expression which is simple and easy to follow, His Holiness touches on every aspect of our daily lives. When applied and practised with sincerity, this teaching will develop an individual's warm-hearted compassion. It enriches the quality of life and gives meaning to this human existence. Studying this text leads us to feel that His Holiness is speaking directly to each one of us, and it is universal in its application.

This English translation has been prepared by Acharya Nyima Tsering, who has put in many months of arduous and painstaking labour, with love, to produce a work of excellent quality. I rejoice in the merit thus gained by him. In addition, many learned scholars have been involved in contributing their skills to the production of this work.

What little merit has been accrued through publishing this book is dedicated to the welfare of all sentient beings.

Gyatsho Tshering
Director

April, 1995

Translator's Note

Although all sentient beings try to achieve happiness and eliminate suffering by means of physical, verbal and mental activities, out of an inability to conceive the right method and path they mistake suffering for happiness and essenceless things as having essence. Because of such misapprehensions, they find themselves in perpetual misery. With this in mind and in order to lead sentient beings out of samsara and into the blissful state, His Holiness the XIV Dalai Lama—the incontrovertible emanation of Avalokiteshvara (Lord of Compassion)—with deep love and compassion for all the migratory beings of this degenerate time, gave this oral teaching on Ngulchu Gyalsas Thogmed Zangpo's Thirty Seven Practices of a Bodhisattva, at Bodh Gaya in the year 1974.

The Tibetan text was carefully transcribed by Research Officer Mr Tashi Tsering in the first instance and later by Assistant Editor Mr Wangdu Tsering. It was skilfully and thoroughly examined and edited by the eminent scholars Ven. Doboom Rinpoche, Ven. Dagyab Rinpoche, Ven. T.C. Tara and Ven. Lati Rinpoche. My heartfelt thanks go to them all for their painstaking efforts, which provided the basis for my subsequent translation of the work into English. I am also extremely grateful to our Director, Mr Gyatsho Tshering, for his altruistic intention in supporting this translation project and his consistent encouragement during its process. I am indebted to Vyvyan Cayley and Mike Gilmore for editing the translated work and to Professor Jay Garfield and Dr Paul Nietupski, both of whom offered valuable suggestions for improvements to the translation. For the sake of readability in the English language, and to transform a spoken discourse into its written form, the text has been edited and condensed without altering the meaning in any way.

Special thanks go to my spiritual master Ven. Professor Samdhong Rinpoche, who at my request kindly spared so much of his precious time to edit the translation in fine detail. Gratitude is also due to all my teachers, Ven. Professor Yeshi Thapkey, Ven. Thupten Tsering and others, for giving me valuable teachings and affectionate guidance. Without the help of these great teachers I would have been unable to bring out this work. My thanks also go to Ven. Khamtrul Rinpoche, Geshe Drubthob, Ven. Gen Lobsang Gyatso, Kirti Tsenshap Rinpoche and Gen Lamrimpa for their discussions with me on the profundities of Buddhist philosophy.

Last but not least, I extend my appreciation to my family members for their unstinting co-operation and support.

Acharya Nyima Tsering
Translator

DAY ONE

Introductory Talk

We have gathered together in Bodh Gaya in order to perform the Kalachakra initiation. You have come from many different areas, motivated by your faith. Owing to poor transportation you have endured a tiring journey, but still you have overlooked your fatigue to gather here.

We shall be performing a great initiation later on. But first, there are many people here who have mere faith in the Dharma without any true understanding of it. They have no experience of hearing and listening to the Dharma, and so do not know its actual meaning. During the initiation itself there will be no time to give a lengthy explanation. So if we just let this time go to waste, no good will be accomplished in return for the hardship and expense involved in getting here.

The purpose of our gathering here is to listen to the Dharma and receive an initiation in order to transform our minds. For our way of thinking is the main cause for attaining, and condition for maintaining, a positive mental disposition. In a few exceptional cases a positive disposition is innate in the mind, but these are rare. So it may be helpful if I spend the first few days explaining the general meaning of Dharma. I feel that short and interesting sessions should be given so that we don't all get tired.

Today I shall begin this general explanation, and in particular I shall include an introduction to the Mahayana teachings. I shall be teaching by oral transmission the Thirty Seven Practices of a Bodhisattva composed by Ngulchu Gyalsas Thogmed Zangpo, which presents essential advice for the Bodhisattva practice.

The Vinaya states that when listening to the Dharma one should neither sit on a chair nor stand, nor wear shoes, hat or turban, nor hold a weapon or an umbrella. An exception can be made to some of these rules in the event of sickness. The Lord Buddha said, in the discipline of the Dharma:

2

If it happens that sick people have to sell all the ornaments of the Buddha's image, spiritual texts and stupas in order to survive, then they should do it.

This exception is made because the Buddhadharma is based on compassion. In fact, compassion is its root. So this applies here today. Though people may not yet be sick, there is a chance that they may fall sick because of the scorching sun. Therefore, wearing a hat or putting up an umbrella are allowed. Similarly, those monks who do not have a hat may use part of their robes to cover their heads.

Good sanitation should be observed, appropriate to the climate, and good behaviour according to the country, place and weather conditions. Those who have overcome the four internal elements do not have to rely on the external elements. But since we have not conquered the internal elements we should act in accordance with the powerful external elements.

Before giving teachings in our tradition we recite the mantra for suppressing or uprooting evil, and also the Heart Sutra to remove obstacles. This is so that we do not experience the hindrances resulting from evil forces or from those who lead others astray whilst listening to and teaching the Dharma. Today we shall recite the Heart Sutra to eradicate obstacles, and after that I would like to start off the prayers by reciting the Manjushri puja three times; then I'll start the supplication to Manjushri.

O compassionate one, by the rays of your omniscient mind...

Then we'll offer a supplication mandala and after finishing this mandala, in order to merge the motivation of guru and disciple, we have to go for refuge by reciting the refuge prayer three times, and generate the altruistic mind. The refuge prayer is:

I go for refuge to the Buddha, Dharma and Sangha Until I attain enlightenment.

We go for refuge with these two lines. After that we usually dedicate the merit which we will accumulate through generosity and listening to and teaching the Dharma. The person who gives teachings recites, "The merit which I accumulate by giving teachings..." and the listeners recite, "The merit which I accumulate by listening to the Dharma..." thus changing the words accordingly. We should also include this dedication: "With this wholesome merit, may all the accumulated wholesome deeds of the three times become a cause of gaining the highest state of enlightenment." This is generating bodhicitta in the form of supplication or prayer.

You have all made a strong commitment to come to Bodh Gaya for these teachings. You have not come here thinking about the food and drink to be served to you, nor the great show to be seen here, nor because by coming here you will gain fame and a high reputation. You have come to receive Dharma teachings, including the teachings of Mahayana, tantra, highest yoga tantra and the glorious Kalacakra initiation of Lord Buddha. So you have come here for a good purpose and have put tireless effort into receiving these Dharma teachings. If someone from the outside views this, they might consider all this effort to be in vain. But when we look at the purpose and reasoning behind it, it is extremely beneficial.

Even if you do not forsake this worldly life to pursue the Dharma, making an effort such as this indicates that a sacrifice is being made for the sake of the Dharma and is a sign of strong determination. What is the purpose behind such tireless effort and strong determination? The purpose, or benefit, and the essence of seeking the Dharma is that all sentient beings share a feeling of 'I' and an innate longing for happiness and peace, as well as a desire to avoid unhappiness and suffering.

This kind of feeling is experienced even by small insects. In the case of human beings, we can see that whether people come from the east, west, middle or border of their country and whether their skin is black, yellow or white, all seek happiness and the avoidance of unhappiness.

In our minds we may express the thought, "May I have happiness," even though we do not understand this feeling of 'I' clearly. On the basis of this experience of 'I', we have such thoughts as, "May I be happy; may I not face difficulty; may I live long and not die; may I have a good livelihood with plenty of food and clothing." So everything comes back to the 'I'. After that, we think of 'my' relatives, 'my' country.

4

This is the same for every human being, and is also true for all creatures down to tiny insects. They don't have broad minds and intelligence, nor do they possess the varieties of thoughts that we humans do. But still they have the feeling of 'I' and they can feel, "May I be happy," or "I'm in great danger; may I be free from this danger." So all beings have the same desires, such as the desire for happiness and aversion to suffering. To have these desires is our right, it is reasonable, and they can often be accomplished. We rely on different methods in pursuit of these goals, to suit our individual capacities and to deal with the varying degrees of suffering to be eliminated and of happiness to be gained.

Happiness and suffering can be dependent upon the body or the mind. Moreover, they can depend upon body or mind in the short-term or the long-term, not only in this life but also in the next lifetime. As far as this life is concerned, we can reflect on the benefits of childhood through to old age; in terms of the present moment, we can think of the long-term benefits related to today and tomorrow.

Although insects have similar thoughts of happiness and suffering as human beings, their ability to seek happiness and eliminate suffering is temporary and covers a short span. They cannot think of the future in terms of the next five, 10 or 30 years nor recall the time when they were young. But we human beings think about accomplishing happiness and eliminating suffering not only for today, tomorrow and the day after tomorrow, but through our whole lifetime. We also look beyond ourselves to contemplate the happiness of our relatives and friends, and further to our country and the whole world.

Thus, seeking happiness and eliminating suffering involves beings of different capabilities in different ways. Some people accomplish great things and others lesser things. Generally speaking, compared with animals we human beings have an extensive range of kinds of happiness we try to attain and sufferings we try to eradicate. From the time when humankind came into being up to now, we have spent our lives pursuing these aims, although we may not have been aware that we were involved in such a pursuit from the moment of our birth. During childhood we may have experienced some temporary happiness, after which we sought more of the same. For instance, we may have told a small lie, such as one to receive sweets or gifts, and we involved ourselves completely in such a small purpose in order to experience a little happiness and avoid a little suffering. Gradually, as we grew older, our suffering and happiness became more broad-ranging and deeper and so more difficulties arose.

The most important method of seeking happiness and eliminating suffering is to increase knowledge, and so we make progress by establishing schools. And in these schools different subjects are taught, including languages. Languages have many words and convey many meanings on many different topics. The mind which governs all this should be very sharp and be able to think in many different ways; we give education precisely in order to develop such sharp brains which are vast and broad-minded.

There is also the suffering of the body to try to avoid. Hospitals have been established to treat the many different diseases. Likewise, the purpose of eating and drinking, and of working—whether it be farming work, industrial labour or whatever—is to seek happiness and eliminate suffering. In today's world we find a whole range of customs and systems, constitutions and policies, monetary standards and views, yet all have the same aim of seeking happiness and eliminating suffering and are simply different aspects and methods.

Among these, differing views have come into existence because people began to explore this issue somewhat more deeply. Various methods intended to bring about happiness and eradicate suffering have been established as a result of such analytical exploration. One is the formation of the Communist Party. Communists say that the main cause of human suffering is inequality of wealth among the different sectors or classes of society. The redistribution of wealth, therefore, is the method that Communists work with in order to gain happiness for people and eliminate their suffering. This is just one view.

Among all the views which exist, there are those which do not stop at merely exploring the ways to bring about temporary happiness and relieve short-term suffering. Holders of these views begin by exploring these temporary causes and conditions, looking at the arising of that temporary cause and condition and then at the cause of the cause, and the cause of that cause, and so on, like links in a chain. By thinking and investigating deeply we arrive at the view of Dharma.

6

We can contemplate various aspects of suffering and happiness —how these sufferings came to us; how happiness arises in a broad sense; how and where this world came into existence and depending on what cause; what the purpose and benefit is of life in this world (for whether there is a benefit or not, the world still came into existence based on its previous existence); what the future will hold and what the individual person can do about it, and what he or she thinks about it. Thinking constructively about these things means that we cannot just depend on what we see with our eyes and hear with our ears, but we must go deeper into the subject.

Some people attribute the existence of the world and human beings to God, saying that this is all His creation. There are many explanations apart from this one, also, some of which are based on reasoning and others not. Thus, some people establish philosophical tenets with the statement that, "This is reasonable and that is not," while others do not have such profound thoughts but spend their lives earning a living, relying on temporary happiness and the temporary avoidance of suffering. Of these two, one type of person is a tenet holder and one is a non-tenet holder. Within the tenet holders there are two kinds, the tenet holders of the external (non-Buddhist) and internal (Buddhist) views.

When dealing with this profound subject, of how to find happiness and eliminate suffering, in relation to the body we can see that the focus is the necessities of food and clothing, with their secondary aspects of housing, bedding and other material facilities. But it soon becomes clear that it is not enough just to be able to find enough food to fill our stomachs. When we explore the suffering and happiness of the body more deeply, we find that although they are strong experiences, comparatively speaking the happiness and suffering of the mind are more powerful. Someone may have a healthy body and ample food and drink, but if he has an unhappy mind he may become crazy and even commit suicide. Some people who become extremely wealthy are always tense; they breathe heavily and frequently talk of being unsatisfied and unhappy.

Conversely, we can observe people who remain calm and happy even when there is a scarcity of food and drink. If we have mental happiness and quietude, then it is quite easy to bear the sufferings of the body. If our minds are too tense, however, immediately upon receiving one possession we want another and there is a great deal of expectation involved. When something goes slightly wrong, we cannot bear it. A mind like this, with no strong endurance, will always be dissatisfied even if the person lives in very good circumstances. So we can see that the mind is of prime importance, and that we can eliminate mental suffering and derive mental happiness through our own way of thinking.

That is why people face similar circumstances in different ways. For example, we may find two patients in a hospital, one of whom accepts the Dharma and has faith in the law of cause and effect, and the other who has no thoughts on this karmic relationship and becomes agitated, trying to eliminate the momentary suffering. In Tibetan we say, 'broken mouth, torn nose'—which means that bad things happen to both of them—yet one of them feels completely helpless and, being unable to endure the suffering, cries out in pain. The other is tormented by similar suffering yet rarely expresses it, maintaining a calm and courageous attitude.

As an example we can look at the Tibetan people: at this time in our history we have been deprived of our homeland and have been scattered throughout the world, and there is definitely unhappiness about this in our community. On top of that we have become refugees and have to rely on other people. Yet, although we face these difficulties, our minds are quite calm and, it seems, quite well satisfied. It is nearly 15 years since we became refugees and now, generally speaking, there are few problems to be seen. Many of the Tibetan people who have gathered here for the teachings seem well off, and the majority of the Tibetan people coming from Bhutan, India and Sikkim who attended yesterday's audience were colourfully dressed, even though as refugees we don't possess a place of our own that is the size of the palm of our hand.

The fact that despite living in such difficult and tense circumstances we have stayed well off is partly due to people's talents and mental acuity. But in another way it depends upon our merits, both greater and lesser. Owing to our merits we have not fallen into a helpless situation and things go relatively smoothly. Looking from the broader perspective, this period in Tibet's history is not a hopeless

8

one. It is rather a case of we, as Tibetans, encountering a temporary obstacle. We have not used up our merit; it has been caught like Rahula caught the sun and moon. This happened very suddenly, but it is not the end and there is hope of increasing our merit. So all of us must generate great courage, accomplish as many wholesome deeds as we can, accumulate merit and have good hearts. Gaining merit is important and extremely powerful.

Similarly, I have a strong intention because of my youth to live for many years. We should all have such strength of mind in order to live for a long time and our attitude should be one of generating courage, as I am doing. You elderly monks shouldn't become depressed or discouraged, although you are ageing and your hair has either gone white or you have become bald. Generally speaking, your merit will offer support.

These are all side topics, and my main point is this: although we are facing much trouble and controversy, still there is hope and tranquillity in our minds. Having a calm mind while facing difficulties is wholly profitable. It doesn't mean that by practising the Dharma we will immediately eliminate starvation and thirst or increase our available amount of food and drink. But by thinking of the Dharma we experience tranquillity and that tranquillity gives us pleasure. This is worthwhile, isn't it?

So regardless of whether there is life after death, cause and effect and the Triple Gem or not, during our lifetime and in our day-to-day life we should keep our inner mind calm and not make trouble for our friends. It is very good to maintain a sense of humour, bring benefit to others and spend our life in this manner. Also, when we wake early in the morning, we should be aware of the possibility that something bad might happen to us today. Then if something bad does happen, our minds will be well prepared and we will be able to maintain an even state of mind. Before we go to sleep at night we should reflect on the good preparations we made by thinking such thoughts in the morning. Otherwise, if we expect to be calm and happy every day and think only from the positive side, our minds become disturbed when something unpleasant happens or we meet a person with whom we do not feel comfortable, and we have a restless night at the end of that day.

We should have the courage to bear whatever difficult circumstances may arise. If another person inflicts harm on us and we retaliate, maybe we will end up in court; if we allow our friends to get involved in the case there will be problems with expenses and possessions. There is no purpose in causing so much trouble, whereas there is benefit in enduring the problem. Most people are not able to practise in this way and be good-hearted to everyone, showing love to one another and helping one another. If we are able to increase this kind of behaviour in society, then really and truly there is hope for peace in this world.

It is a mistake to pursue the goals of happiness and the avoidance of suffering by deceiving and humiliating other people. We must try to achieve happiness and eliminate suffering by being good-hearted and well-behaved. It is not good to hear of people seeking these goals by misbehaviour and deception, by murder and through wars. But these days in our world people act out of greed and deception, and really are using methods like this to search for happiness.

We have seen great material progress in the world, but big countries continue to humiliate small countries and many deaths occur as a result. Though they may believe they will find happiness and eliminate suffering in this way, actually there is more fighting, more famine, more deception, more tension and altogether more suffering endured by oppressed people in the 20th century.

This isn't happening because of scarcity of food or lack of facilities. Schools and hospitals have been developed, housing and transportation improved, food and drink supplies increased. But truth and honesty have been lost in society and that is why there is less happiness. Those with wealth and power can do whatever they want, whereas one who is truthful and honest but has no power or wealth will have no success.

These kinds of examples are prevalent in society today, which is very sad, and such global mistaken values have also caused misfortune to fall upon Tibet. These days everyone is talking about peace and truth, from China and India to the Western countries. But in actual fact, the sufferings of oppressed people come about because of the mistaken notions which are behind the way our societies function.

10

So we return to that which is called the Dharma. Dharma should not be practised only by people living in remote countries, by barbarians whose views are narrow. It should also be practised by open and broad-minded people. But there's nothing wonderful about the construction of temples and monasteries per se, nor about prostrations, circumambulation and offerings in themselves. Indeed, it's doubtful as to whether that is in fact Dharma. If inside our mind there is positive energy, then that is Dharma. If there is negative energy, that is not Dharma.

Dharma should be in our heart. If our mind is tamed, calm and relaxed, we are practising Dharma. If someone wears a robe and speaks of the three baskets of Dharma but does not have a tamed mind, he is not a Dharma practitioner. Whoever has Dharma is very open-minded, relaxed, humble and calm and naturally has a good heart; whereas he who deceives and belittles people and tells lies is not engaged in Dharma practice. The kind of behaviour that really is Dharma practice consists of refraining from falsehood and abiding by the truth, neither humiliating nor mocking others, being humble and adopting a lowly position, having a good heart, helping others and sacrificing self.

Even those who do not accept the theory of rebirth and so forth may analyse to see whether we need Dharma in this very lifetime or not and then they will know. We want to be happy ourselves, and we want our friends to be happy. Yet even though we may have ample food and drink at present, there is an uneasiness in our minds and we have to live with this feeling. We may begin to fall out with our friends, to deceive and bully them and put them down. In the short-term we may gain wealth and material possessions in this way, and be able to put on good clothes, wear a nice watch, eat good food and drink good tea. But we will not be happy if all this wealth and these possessions have come about through bullying, humiliating and deceiving other people.

Perhaps it will prey on our minds that our actions may land us in court. Because we are the one with wealth and power right now, our friends may use respectful words in front of us. They may speak of our good qualities as being even greater than those of Lord Buddha. But behind our back they will be cursing us and saying things like, "May he die very badly," and we can hardly find anyone who likes us. So if we have to live in this way, even though we may have plenty to eat and drink, where is our happiness to be found? In the depths of our mind we will be unhappy.

Whether or not our conduct is known by others, if when we are about to die we feel that we have lived our lives in a bad way, then we will be very unhappy. The wealth we have accumulated by misconduct cannot be carried with us. We may have a big house but that must be left behind. We may have authentic savings in the bank with a certificate to prove it, but at the time of death we have no use for that money. We have to leave our close relatives, parents and others who care for us behind. Worse than this, we have to leave our own bodies.

So any wealth accumulated by misconduct in this lifetime will not bring benefit at the time of death and may even cause problems, such as worrying about who will take care of our possessions after our death. Or we may become anxious when we are dying, fearing that our good-hearted relatives will end up fighting each other in order to get their hands on that wealth. Isn't it bad if we have to end our life in this way?

However, if we are good-mannered, with a kind nature and a good heart, staying calm and relaxed, benefitting others and always regarding ourself as lower than them, we can withstand a temporary scarcity of food and drink and can usually make good friends with everyone, and they become like our relatives. Then when we face difficulties it is likely that someone will help us.

We Buddhists believe in life after death, and it can be proven by reasoning. So we should analyse with an open mind, thinking deeply about our experience. There definitely is life after death. Because of this fact, the collective karma of sentient beings has brought about the environmental result of the world in general, and our individual karma has brought about the facilities that we enjoy. If there is no life after death, we would have to say that this world came into existence without a cause—there could be no other explanation.

We will also experience happiness in the next lifetime if we live in a kind and compassionate way now, so we can feel at ease about that. But on the other hand, how much suffering will we have to undergo in this and the next lifetime if we indulge in misconduct?

12

This is therefore a valid reason for engaging in Dharma practice. In short, being good-hearted and polite brings happiness; being rude causes many bad things to happen.

There are those in the world today who do not believe in Dharma and criticise it. So it is up to us to explain Dharma well and then there will be no grounds for criticism. The good example set by a Dharma practitioner, who acts with a good heart and compassionate mind towards sentient beings and society in general, can be recognised and accepted by everyone, whether or not they believe in life after death. From the point of view of this lifetime only, having a good heart and benefitting others are proper attitudes for everyone, whether they are Dharma practitioners or not.

So the essence of Dharma is generating a good heart, and the complete explanation of how to generate a good heart is given in the Mahayana teachings. This Buddhist teaching has arisen in the kalpa of a thousand Buddhas. Among the Buddhas who have already appeared, the fourth, Shakyamuni Buddha, is well known in this present world. In this Arya land of India and in this very spot of Bodh Gaya, Shakyamuni Buddha became enlightened 2,500 years ago. He made the first turning of the wheel of the Dharma in Varanasi and gave many Dharma teachings up until he attained parinirvana. He elucidated various aspects of Dharma in the human and deva realms, as well as underground, on the ground and above the ground, to common followers, to the small group of uncommon followers and to the uncommon, inconceivable secret followers. He gave varied and intensive, profound Dharma teachings in this way.

If condensed, they fall into two vehicles, of which Mahayana is higher than Hinayana in the field of thought that is mind generation and in the conduct of the six perfections, and the result of this practice is the three emanation bodies. The Mahayana teaching is supreme in the various aspects of conduct. Within Mahayana there exist sutra and tantra, of which tantra is higher. Therefore, the union of sutra and tantra teachings is extremely precious. This is the kind of Dharma that flourished in India and was transferred to Tibet, the Land of Snows.

The Buddhist teachings also spread northwards, to Mongolia and many other places which until recently we knew as being part of

13

the USSR, and eastwards into China, Korea, Japan and so forth. On the western side, the Dharma spread to Afghanistan and several other places. Buddha himself predicted that the Mahayana teachings would spread 'in a northerly direction', which is said to be from India into Tibet and from the northern side of Tibet into Mongolia.

The Buddhadharma began in India during the lifetime of Shakyamuni Buddha, who was renowned for turning the first dharmachakra which was mainly a teaching based on the Hinayana doctrine. He propounded the Mahayana teachings to some fortunate people, although it seems that these teachings were not all that popular nor well-known during his time. This is why some people in the past, as well as today, have claimed that the Mahayana teachings are not the teachings of the Buddha.

After his parinirvana, the Mahayana teachings degenerated until they remained only in name and this state of affairs lasted for a long time. According to the Buddha's prediction, Nagarjuna and Asanga laid the foundations for the resurgence of Mahayana, and the Mahayana teachings flourished for many centuries after that. Then both the Mahayana and Hinayana doctrines gardually waned in the Arya land of India until it seemed as if the teachings had disappeared completely.

In Tibet, meanwhile, there were many ups and downs from the arrival of the Dharma up until 1959, but the Buddhadharma never died out without a trace in our country. The Dharma degenerated during the time of Langdarma, and that period lasted for about 80 years. But even that only happened in U-Tsang, the central part of Tibet, and the Dharma remained active in the regions around this central area. After that there was some waxing and waning in the spread of the Dharma, but the combined teachings of sutra and tantra have been well preserved in Tibet for 1,000 years.

The chronological development proceeded in Tibet from the Nyingma (old) to the Sarma (new) sects. Within the Sarma there were the Sakya, Kagyud, Kadam, Jonang and Gedenpa (or Gelugpa). Through these sects, many different names and techniques developed, as well as many ways of elaborating the teachings of sutra and tantra and means of holding the instructions of the respective lamas of these schools. There are slight differences in procedure, but all are the same in the unified teaching of sutra and tantra, which became

14

highly developed in Tibet. Because of this, the neighbouring areas of Bhutan, Sikkim, Ladakh, Mon (Arunachal Pradesh) and Mongolia became students of Tibetan religious culture. These days the Tibetan teachers are refugees while the disciples remain comfortably settled; but today teacher and disciples are gathered here together.

The teachings of the Buddha we are practising, which consist of the union of sutra and tantra, are extremely pure and beneficial. Bodhicitta and a good heart, which are explained in the sutras, are the very foundation. Tantra becomes mere dry words if we do not have bodhicitta and there is no special nor profound result to be gained from studying it. Similarly, both Mahayana and Hinayana are explained in the sutrayana. If the profound view of emptiness—which is skilfully presented in the Mahayana teachings—is absent, tantra becomes ineffective and cannot result in any realisation.

As explained in the sutras, precious bodhicitta which cherishes others more dearly than oneself has compassion and love as its root. And the view of emptiness, which is that all phenomena lack inherent existence and are pure from the very beginning, is also explained therein. If we lack experiential knowledge of the union of these two, bodhicitta and emptiness, then we do not gain results from practising the profound Dharma of tantra.

Therefore, we must keep renunciation, bodhicitta and right view as the foundation, as explained in the sutras. From the point of view of highest yoga tantra, we have to base the generation stage and the completion stage on this foundation. If we do this, profound and extensive results will occur, as is explained in the tantric texts and their respective commentaries.

There is no benefit in such profound instructions without that foundation, even though there may be the generation and completion stages, channels, winds and drops, etc. We have to turn into a proper vessel to receive the teachings, just as we must be able to stand up to strong medicine prescribed for us and not have too weak a constitution to tolerate it. So we must know the three principal aspects of the path—renunciation, bodhicitta and right view—in order to practise tantra, and then think and shape our mind properly. Then the practise of tantra becomes the union of sutra and tantra.

The life force on any path, whether it be sutra or tantra, is precious bodhicitta. Therefore it is extremely important.

I will now begin a brief transmission and explanation of the Thirty Seven Practices of a Bodhisattva, composed by the Tibetan scholar Ngulchu Gyalsas Thogmed Zangpo. There is no time to go into an extensive biography of him now, but he was a contemporary of Buton Thamchad Khyenpa (Buton Rinpoche), by whom he was well respected and trusted. It is said that at one time Buton Rinpoche had an affliction in his hand and he requested the author, saying, "You have bodhicitta in your heart, therefore bless my hand." There were many disciples who sought teachings from both Buton Rinpoche and Thogmed Zangpo.

Whatever view he holds, merely by looking at his text we can know that Thogmed Zangpo embodies bodhicitta, and so this instruction is extremely beneficial. Bodhisattvas can be known by their natural signs, just as invisible fire can be inferred through smoke and water can be inferred through seeing a heron. By reading this text we understand the suitability of the title Bodhisattva for Thogmed Zangpo.

Thogmed Zangpo had a fox which he usually kept close by him, like a pet dog. Because Thogmed Zangpo himself was extremely calm and good-hearted, the fox also became good-hearted. It didn't hurt anybody and also didn't eat meat. Thogmed Zangpo's mind was so sensitive that he would invariably weep when giving teachings. Some disciples said that whenever the omniscient Buton Rinpoche was giving teachings they would always be laughing and whenever Thogmed Zangpo was giving teachings they would always be crying.

Thogmed Zangpo became a great scholar by studying extensively during his earlier life and he composed commentaries on the great treatises. He made bodhicitta the main object of his practice during his later life, and he became a great scholar and practitioner through concentrating solely on bodhicitta.

I received the oral transmission of the Thirty Seven Practices of a Bodhisattva and teachings on this from the Khunu Lama Tenzin Gyaltsen Rinpoche. He received it from an extremely great renunciant practitioner, a Nyingma lama from a Dzogchen monastery in eastern Tibet.

16

The Thirty Seven Practices of a Bodhisattva

We begin with the exemplary opening of the text, followed by the actual text, and finally the conclusion. The content of the exemplary offering to the enlightened ones is divided into the salutation and the pledge to compose the text:

> Namo Arya Lokeshvara.
> I always respectfully prostrate through my three doors[1]
>   to the
> Supreme guru and protector Lokeshvara, who although seeing
> All phenomena as devoid of going and coming,
> Endeavours one-pointedly to benefit sentient beings.

By saying, "Namo Arya Lokeshvara", the author is making an offering to the guru and protector Avalokiteshvara. The Buddha and Bodhisattvas in general are not mentioned here, but special mention is made of the guru and Avalokiteshvara (Chenrezig), which indicates that this text reveals the practice of the Bodhisattvas.

Since the root of bodhicitta is compassion and great compassion is itself the root of generating a resolute intention, by relying upon it bodhicitta will be generated. Avalokiteshvara is the manifested body of compassion of all the enlightened beings, or Buddhas, and therefore the author makes specific offerings to him. Likewise he does so to the supreme guru because, in the words of Jowo Je Palden Atisha, "All the major and minor great qualities are generated by relying on the lama." This means that all the wholesome qualities in general, especially the qualities of the Mahayana, emerge through having confidence in the guru.

The root of the path of Mahayana is love and, most particularly, bodhicitta based on compassion. All the methods of practising bodhicitta which appear in the treatise of Shantideva, such as equalising and exchanging self and others, are the practices of Bodhisattvas with extremely strong minds and are to be developed by relying on the guru. This is the reason for particular obeisance being made to the guru.

If one wonders about the qualities with which such a lama and Avalokiteshvara are endowed, the answer is that they are perfect in abandonment of afflictions and in realisation. This also entails the simultaneous realisation of the two truths. If we are unable to uproot and abandon the afflictions and the obscurations to enlightenment, we cannot perceive the two truths simultaneously. It would then be impossible to benefit migratory beings wholeheartedly, based on an unwavering and complete understanding of all phenomena as emptiness. Therefore, we make prostration to such a guru and Avalokiteshvara, who are endowed with these qualities and who express the qualities of the Buddha, perfect in abandonment and realisation.

As is stated in the salutation stanza of the root text of Mulamadhyamikakarika:

> Although seeing all phenomena as devoid of going and coming...

All the conventional phenomena of dependent origination which arise and dissolve are in the nature of suchness, which means that ultimately they are free from the eight different aspects of dependent arising, such as being born and ceasing, coming and going and so forth.

The state of mind that does not waver even for a moment from that non-conceptual mental equipoise in which subject and object are inseparable, and in which there is not even the slightest interference from the subtle dualistic mind, can be compared to pouring water into water. With such an unwavering state of mind, we emanate different forms in a hundred or a thousand places throughout the various pure and impure mundane realms.

If the conditions gather in sentient beings, the activities of the enlightened ones will invariably benefit them. Therefore we should go for refuge to the enlightened Avalokiteshvara and do so not only when bad circumstances occur. The author says that he will always prostrate from the three doors of body, speech and mind with respect, from this day onwards.

18

Next comes the promise to compose the text:

> The perfected Buddhas, the source of all benefits and
> pleasures,
> Arise from having practised the holy Dharma.
> As accomplishing this also depends on knowing its prac-
> tices,
> I shall explain the practice of the Bodhisattvas.

Our karma is the ultimate source from which all sufferings and happiness arise, happiness from good karma and suffering from bad karma. Since the causes of suffering are the faults of the mind, these faults should be eliminated; while the causes of pleasure, like good moral behaviour and good qualities, should be increased. If we analyse in depth, we see that the way to increase good qualities and therefore happiness is to engage in the Dharma, for the source of all benefits and happiness is the teaching of the Buddha.

Therefore, as stated in the 'Nga rim chenmo' (Great Exposition of Secret Mantra) by Je Rinpoche (Lama Tsong Khapa):

> The source of benefit and happiness of all migratory
> beings,
> Including devas, is only the Buddha's teachings. By trusting
> in this,
> Uphold the holy Dharma with great strength and
> Determination, even at the cost of your life.

We can become fully enlightened, completely endowed with all good qualities and free from all negativities if we practise according to the Dharma. Then a spontaneous overflow of virtuous activities will occur and, by displaying the mystical dance of revealing various aspects according to each sentient being's disposition and faith, we can benefit others spontaneously without effort. Such results of the highest state of enlightenment arise from practising the holy Dharma, and in this way the Dharma can be seen to be the source of all benefits and happiness.

By practising this Dharma, the previous Buddhas became free from all faults and endowed with all good qualities, perfected their own purpose and accomplished the purpose of others spontaneously and effortlessly. Remembering the purpose of gaining enlightenment and the qualities and benefits of the Dharma, we should put it into practice and not restrict ourselves to mere intellectual knowledge gained through listening to it.

Knowing only one word of Dharma and putting that into practice brings profound and special results; whereas those who can recite from memory 100,000 texts but don't practise the Dharma won't experience all that much benefit. Therefore, special mention is made of the purpose of practice at this time.

So we should put the Dharma into practice right now if we are seeking happiness and desire to avoid suffering, if we wish to be free from our faults and to perfect all the positive qualities. The author also explains how to practise the precious bodhicitta of cherishing others more than ourselves, which is the practice of a Bodhisattva.

To proceed to the actual treatise, it seems that if I make a division in accordance with the practices of people of the three different potentials, it begins with an explanation of people of limited scope:

ONE

Now, when the elusive great vessel of leisure and benefi-
    cial circumstances has been obtained,
It is the practice of the Bodhisattvas to listen,
Contemplate and meditate day and night to free
Themselves and others from the ocean of samsara.

In order to practise the Dharma we need to know about it. In order to know about it, we need to hear it. Since this is the time we have obtained a human body, if we listen to and contemplate the Dharma, we will come to know it. We should practise if we are able to do so, for if we are not careful now that we have gained a human birth, what can we do when not in the human state? At present we are teaching and listening to the Dharma. But if we were born as dogs, the state of our bodies would deprive us of the good fortune to hear and practise the Dharma and there would be no chance of leading our minds to it. We would be helpless.

20

But we have been born as human beings, and not only that: among all the human beings, we have been born where the Dharma flourishes. Also, we are able to see with our eyes and hear with our ears and our minds know a little of what is to be abandoned and what is to be adopted. So at this time we have to practise the Dharma by listening, contemplating and meditating. Now, some people are illiterate and can't even read the words of the Dharma. Nevertheless, they have attained a human birth and can therefore make an effort to learn about the Dharma through talking to others, and they can know something according to their capacity.

On becoming old, our powers of recognition become unclear, our senses grow dim and we mumble through our teeth—nonetheless, we have obtained a human body and can make as much effort as we are capable of to understand the Dharma. It is better to take a human body than that of a horse or a dog. At least we can recite 'om mani padme hum'. So this human body is very precious.

However, there is nothing wonderful in merely attaining a human body. There are more than four billion people in this world, yet if we were to count up the number of people who are born into a place where the Dharma flourishes, that number would be very small. Then among them, there are not many who have trust in the Dharma and an opportunity to practise by listening, contemplating and meditating on the union of sutra and tantra. So we should put every effort into our practice without getting depressed and we must take good care not to misuse this good birth. For if we waste our time and yet expect to experience benefit in the future, that is very unwise.

It is difficult to obtain the combination of beneficial circumstances and leisure. Why is this so? Because we must have a complete cause to obtain such circumstances and a human rebirth cannot be attained if the cause is lacking. What is the cause of human rebirth? It is our own accumulated virtue. However, virtuous karma from the past will be expended and needs to be renewed by virtuous actions in the present. For example, if a person once had money but has none now, it's no use going shopping. Similarly, although we may have accumulated virtuous karma previously, it cannot benefit us if we have no virtuous karma in the present.

It is difficult to know whether the potential of virtuous deeds previously accumulated remains with us in the present without degeneration. Some of the virtuous deeds we have accumulated in the past will have arisen from pure preliminary practice, actual practice and concluding practice, and some from impure practices. Strong non-virtuous thoughts, such as anger, destroy the pure practices. Anger is a very powerful eradicator of virtuous deeds and is generated very often, based on major and minor conditions.

We cannot rely on the energy of previous virtuous karma because we are unsure whether it has a positive influence on our lives in the present. So if we try to rely on it, at the time of death we may find rebirth in the human realm extremely difficult. But if we have built up strong virtuous energy in the present we may trust in that. Then even if our lives become hopeless we can expect better circumstances in our next lives.

When we explore our continuum properly, we may find we haven't had an occasion to practise virtuous deeds which can be trusted; alternatively, we may have performed such deeds in the past but we see that they are not powerful enough to rely upon. If this is the case, we should act with great caution. We shouldn't just let our minds relax and expect a good future, because this means we are deceiving ourselves and existing in a vacuum. Instead, it is important for us to behave in a constructive way in our present lives of leisure and freedom.

People may wonder if practising the Dharma necessarily means abandoning our social life and our home and community. Of course, we should definitely practise in this way if it is possible to do so. But there are other ways also in which to practise Dharma. We should try our best to have a kind heart and not engage in misbehaviour, such as lying and stealing, in our day-to-day life; instead, we should be truthful and well-behaved, working to benefit others, lessening our own desire and being contented within ourself. Those who are unable to practise much should still occasionally recite the six-syllable mantra of the compassionate deity Avalokiteshvara, since this is also Dharma.

Our daily life becomes meaningful when we are careful like this. People who are used to behaving badly—such as indulging in laziness,

22

harsh speech, bullying, lying, causing malice and division between people and actively causing harm to others—must try to reduce their involvement in this type of activity from today onwards. Those who are in business should make every effort to be truthful in their dealings with others and refrain from deception and avarice. This is also Dharma.

Some people say: "I am a sinner and so I am unable to practise Dharma." They feel that the Dharma has to be practised in some remote place under conditions too difficult for them. But if one is an evil being one still does not want to experience suffering, such as starvation, thirst and cold, and one wishes to find happiness, so that it is meaningless to put up these obstacles to practice.

Generally speaking, it's rare to find someone who is not a sinner. By this I mean that when we use the word 'sinner' it does not necessarily mean murderer. For my own example, I have taken the Dharma robes and still different negative conceptual thoughts arise in my mind, such as jealousy of those in higher places, competitive feelings with equals and feelings of superiority and teasing those who are lower. These disturbing thoughts will be revealed in my way of talking and my facial expressions if I let them dwell in my mind, and they will be the cause of much negativity, especially if I generate negative thoughts such as a self-cherishing attitude. Because I have taken the bodhicitta vow and have committed myself to tantric practice, such actions will generate many serious negativities.

So we should not be discouraged by thinking of ourselves as sinners, but should try to become better people. I am now around 38 or 39 years old and I intend to check my mind in daily life, in order to make sincere efforts to improve myself during my remaining years. When I reflect back on the past, it seems that some improvement has taken place. As is said in the oral sayings of the Kadampa lineage of geshes: "How can improvement occur? Because compositional phenomena are always by nature changing, therefore it is sure that one day improvement will happen." So it is certain that there will be improvement, although it is difficult effortlessly to arouse renunciation and bodhicitta.

There are different ways of looking at the practice of Dharma. If we look at it one way, the minds of worldly people and the holy Dharma are polarised, as the saying goes: "Ordinary people's minds and the holy Dharma are extremely far apart." But from another perspective, if we practise the Dharma it is very near to us. We do not have to leave our homes and go far away but can practise every day in ordinary life, without misusing our time even for a single day. This is meaningful practice.

For example, we should not take the attitude while we are circumambulating that we are merely going for a walk, nor should we engage in meaningless prayers such as requesting that we not be afflicted with disease and that our wealth and lifespan may increase. Rather, we should pray in a wholesome way and we should be as good-hearted as possible during the circumambulation period of one or two hours. We may think along the lines of this passage from the Bodhicharyavatara ('Guide to the Bodhisattva's Way of Life'): "May I always be a source of various kinds of livelihood for innumerable sentient beings, like the earth and the sky." It is said that there are many benefits from praying like this while circumambulating. We should also bring the image of the previous great and compassionate Muni (Shakyamuni Buddha) to our minds; remembering his kindness, we should mentally pray to him by saying, "May I follow in your footsteps and generate the inner strength to become like you." Offering such fervent prayers brings immense benefit.

We need to listen to, contemplate and meditate upon the Dharma in order to work towards such a perfected state of mind as the Buddha's. When listening to, contemplating and meditating on the Mahayana teachings in particular we should have the same continuity as flowing water, day and night, not misusing our time even for a moment.

We should first study the aspects about which we know nothing. After gaining knowledge of these we should analyse them again and again, in order to plumb the depths of their meaning. Once we've become convinced of their meaning, we should try to gain experiential knowledge of them within our minds, based on the combination of analytical and placement meditation. Spending one's days and nights in such a way is known as the practice of a Bodhisattva.

TWO

It is the practice of the Bodhisattvas to renounce their
  homelands
Which condition desire like water, wavering towards
  relatives;
Anger like fire, spreading towards enemies; and ignorance,
  creating a
Cloudiness in the mind so one forgets what to accept
  and discard.

Attachment, hatred and ignorance increase alongside each other
when we stay in our fatherland. We form attachments not only to our
relatives and friends but also to our ancestors. These attachments arise
inappropriately, as do hatred and anger. Even if we wish to practise
and recite some mantras, our time is occupied with taking care of
our relatives and friends and countering the aims of our enemies. We
show a nice face and kow-tow to those of higher authority, we bully
those who are downtrodden and deceive those of the same status
with our wealth. These actions all arise from staying in a place where
there are so many objects of attachment and anger.

If we have a small house containing few material possessions, we
don't need to be strongly attached to the idea of supporting our
relatives, nor to feel fierce hatred for our enemies. But we can still
have the attachment that comes from thinking, "This is my house."
Similarly, we can become preoccupied even with small material
objects, thinking how they will benefit us by possessing them. Such
distractions cause us to spend our days wastefully.

A single monk may only have a box and shrine and one or two
holy images of body, speech and mind in his house. However, if he
becomes involved in rearranging these few objects many times he is
distracted by such activity, rather than spending his time reciting
mantras and thinking about the Dharma. Therefore, abandoning
one's fatherland is known as the practice of a Bodhisattva.

The root of attachment, hatred and closed-mindedness is ignorance, and we could say that attachment and hatred are like the ministers
of ignorance. Of these two, hatred is like a brave minister who
subdues the enemy, while attachment is the minister of the treasury

or store-house. When all is said and done, attachment, hatred and ignorance lead us invariably into helplessness and other difficulties.

THREE

It is the practice of Bodhisattvas to remain in remote places where
Afflictions gradually diminish by abandoning disturbing locations,
Where wholesome deeds naturally increase by being undistracted, and
Where clear-mindedness gives rise to conviction in the Dharma.

As this says, simply abandoning our fatherland or country is not the answer. For instance, we are refugees and were forced to abandon our country, but if we remain preoccupied with worldly activities we do not learn from that experience. The main purpose of leaving our fatherland is to have less occasion for the arising of attachment, hatred and ignorance. In this verse the qualities of solitude are explained. There are no objects of distraction in a place of solitude, such as home maintenance, family affairs and the collecting and dispersing of material gains. Likewise, there is no one around us talking of attachments and hatred. We can relax in a place where there is pure water and air, we have simple clothes and there's no stress in our mind from having to take care of our belongings. From the time we get up in the morning there is nothing to distract us from Dharma practice, so we should focus on the Dharma in such a setting.

Many noble beings have attained high realisation on the path by depending upon a place of solitude. So if we get the chance to stay in a hermitage before we die, like an animal living in the wild, it is a magnificent opportunity.

Particularly since we monks are free from family responsibilities, we may look up to and follow the example of the Buddha and his disciples, reducing our attachment to food, clothing and fame and challenging the afflictions. We are not achieving anything wonderful just by changing our external dress and wearing symbols. The sign of

26

a monk is that when he abruptly rises from his seat, there is nothing he needs to gather up from that place. If several people have to help him carry his luggage when he is shifting from one location to another, then I do not think he represents the monkhood well.

FOUR

It is the practice of Bodhisattvas to renounce this life,
   since
Relatives and friends of long-standing must part, wealth
   and material goods
Accumulated with great effort must be left behind and
   the body,
Like a guest-house, must be discarded by the guest of
   consciousness.

We are true Dharma practitioners if we seek a solitary place and are able to renounce this worldly life. In order to renounce worldly life, we should look upon this life as essenceless, the ultimate reasons for such a view being impermanence and death. All of us have to die sooner or later. If we have practised Dharma and developed good-heartedness, then at the time of death the future circumstances look hopeful. Otherwise, even if all the people of the world were to be our friends and relatives it would not benefit us at such a time, because we must go alone, leaving all of them behind. A very wealthy person, for example, who owns a chain of factories must leave all those factories behind when he dies.

From the time we were born out of our mother's womb until now we have cherished our bodies so devotedly by saying 'my body', but this doesn't benefit us in the end because we must also leave this body behind. Even as far as the Dalai Lama is concerned, when the day of death of the Dalai Lama comes then of course one has to leave the body of Tenzin Gyatso. There's no way in which body and mind can go together. Usually, if deprived of his blessed robe ('cho gos nam jar')[2], Tenzin Gyatso will experience a downfall, but at the time of death one has to leave this holy robe behind without any downfall.

The time of our death is uncertain. Making plans would be worthwhile if we could trust in a fixed lifespan, but we cannot trust in the duration of our life because we don't know when we will die. We are all together here in this Dharma session today, but some of us may die tonight. We cannot be sure that we will all meet again in tomorrow's session. I cannot give you a 100% guarantee that I won't die tonight, for example.

So if we remain clinging to this life even for one day we are misusing our time, and in this way we can waste months and years on end. Because we don't know when our lives will finish, we should stay mindful and well prepared. Then, even if we die tonight, we will do so without regret. If we die tonight, the purpose of being well prepared is borne out; if we don't die tonight there is no harm in being well prepared, because it will still benefit us.

The physical activity of this lifetime may be observed and understood and things have a way of working themselves out in time. For instance, we experienced a great deal of uneasiness and frustration when we first escaped from Tibet and came to India, wondering how we would survive. In this process of fleeing from one human nation to another human nation, we found that gradually everything worked out.

But when we leave the world of humans, we do so without a protector or supporter and the total responsibility falls on us. We only have our own intelligence to rely on at that time, so we must expend our own effort in order to protect ourselves. As the Buddha said, "I have shown you the path to liberation; know that liberation depends on you." We must put strenuous effort into gaining freedom from the lower migrations, liberation from samsara, freedom from conventional existence and solitary salvation.

It is difficult for the devas to protect us when we go to the next life, so we should be cautious and become as well prepared now as we can. We should place emphasis on future lifetimes rather than clinging to this lifetime only, so that we are able to sacrifice or renounce this life. This is stated in order to establish the essencelessness of this life.

The body is compared to a guest-house, in that it is a place to stay for just a short time and not permanently. At present the guest of consciousness is staying in the guest-house of the body, like renting a place to stay. When the day comes for the consciousness to leave, then

28

the guest-house of the body must be left behind. Not being attached to friends, the body, wealth and possessions is the practice of the Bodhisattvas.

FIVE

It is the practice of Bodhisattvas to abandon non-virtuous
  friends
Who, when associated with, cause the three poisons to
  increase,
The actions of listening, contemplating and meditating to
  diminish,
And love and compassion to become non-existent.

There is a great difference between the qualities we look for in a good lama and close friend, and those we find in a non-spiritual teacher and evil friend. Having access to the former is very beneficial, whereas it is unhelpful to keep company with non-spiritual teachers and evil friends. For even if we wish to become good, by gradually adapting our minds to the bad ways of our friends we may take on their bad habits. This point is said to be extremely important.

The kind of bad or non-spiritual friend we have to forsake is one in whose company we find there is a spontaneous increase in the three afflictions of attachment, hatred and ignorance. Naturally, we are unable to practise the Dharma through listening, contemplating and meditating when in the company of such a friend.

While engaged in Mahayana Dharma practice, such associations will debase the foundation of bodhicitta, which is love and compassion. We should avoid them like we would an epidemic disease.

SIX

It is the practice of Bodhisattvas to hold excellent
  Spiritual friends as even more dear than their own bodies.
When relying on these excellent spiritual friends, faults
  decrease and
Good qualities increase like the waxing of the moon.

This is by way of saying that we should rely upon our lama as the spiritual friend, which Geshe Potawa also states: "There is none superior to the lama in seeking to accomplish liberation. The work of this lifetime can be learned by observation. However, even that is not possible without a teacher. How will you manage without the help of the lama when you suddenly come from the lower migrations to a place where you have never been before?"

Transmuting this flawed mind into a pure state will not occur without much effort being made, and to make such an effort we must know how to direct it and which techniques to use. If we don't know and are not led by an experienced person, the effort will not have the desired result.

Who is that experienced person? It is a qualified lama, who through his experience can show the student the path and let him or her eliminate the obstacles. Just as sick people seek the help of a doctor to be freed from disease, so we should seek the help of a lama to free ourselves from the three delusions. The lama is the person on whom the disciples rely from the depths of their heart.

The lama should not be just anyone. As is said by Dharmaraja Sakya Pandita: "Before starting a small business in buying and selling horses or jewels, one must investigate deeply and ask other people's advice. Similarly, it is not correct to seek teachings on the spot from any person without first analysing the spiritual master, since the Dharma is the only means for achieving the ultimate goal." We should investigate thoroughly in this way to find out whether or not the lama is qualified. We should examine these characteristics of the lama carefully: his adherence to the Vinaya and sutra and his possession of the qualities of a Vajra master, as explained in tantra.

Once we are convinced that he is an appropriate lama, we should rely upon him in the correct way, regarding his knowledge as equal to that of the Buddha and his kindness as superior even to the Buddha's. We should have faith in his qualities and respect him by recollecting his kindness. Holding this respect and his kindness in our mind, we should practise the instructions regarding reliance upon the lama. We should put in sincere effort and make offerings to our lama by practising the Dharma.

30

The best offering we can make to our lama is that of practice. If he is a true, qualified lama, he will be far more pleased with our offering of practice than with any material offerings we may make to him. For instance, Marpa Lotsawa made Milarepa undergo strenuous ascetic practices before eventually allowing him to receive initiation. At that time, Milarepa had no material wealth to offer at all. Another of Marpa's disciples was Ngok Lotsawa, who had material wealth and who offered all he had to his teacher, not even leaving out his broken-legged goat. Marpa sang a song to the effect that he made no distinction between the one who could offer nothing and the one who offered everything. This indicates that he was a qualified lama.

Those who are looking for material gain are not valid Mahayana teachers, as stated by Sharawa, quoted in the Lamrim Chenmo by Tsong Khapa. Relying upon a lama in the proper manner described here is the practice of the Bodhisattvas.

DAY TWO

Introductory Talk

> All three conditional existences are as impermanent as
>   clouds in autumn;
> The birth and death of migratory beings are like observing
>   a dance;
> The life of sentient beings passes as swiftly as lightning in
>   the sky;
> And life moves with the speed of a waterfall from a steep
>   mountain.

This verse from the Gyacher Rolpa sutra describes how all phenomena, including sentient beings and environmental factors, are composed of causes and conditions. Therefore they change from moment to moment and have a perishable, ever-changing nature. There is not one phenomenon which will remain constant.

We can see that our lives as sentient beings are particularly unstable. It is certain that after taking birth we have to die; yet the thought never arises in our minds that death will come to us when the specific external and internal conditions meet, often without warning. All of a sudden death happens to us and we are strolling in the next life, with only our mere name remaining in this world. Such a time will come. Even before this world's history began to be recorded many thousands of years went by, yet we cannot point out a single person in history who has not died. No matter how rich, capable, brave or smart we may be, we none of us can evade death.

Similarly, all parts of the body are temporary and subject to constant change, by nature impermanent, unstable and degenerating. Early in our lives, our eyes are sharp; later when they become dim we have to wear glasses, then gradually even glasses cannot help because of the degeneration of the sense faculty of seeing. Likewise, at an early age we can clearly hear sounds with our ears, but these sounds gradually become more faint until we are deaf and cannot hear anything accurately.

32

If someone is attractive when young so that others like to look upon him or her, that attractiveness can become a source of pride in the body. But gradually, with age, that young and attractive body becomes infirm and bent. Then the very same body feels dirty and even its owner feels revolted by it. Indeed, people may say it is a wonder that someone so old and crooked is still alive, and even the children of that person may be unable to come close without holding their noses. The person himself or herself is afflicted by the suffering of being old and infirm, and feels mentally tired when thinking about the self. Some old people feel like choosing death rather than life. But just by saying, "I prefer to die," death will not come.

When we are young and attractive and have wealth, power, possessions and strength, we are the object of others' respect. Whatever we say is taken as seriously as if it was the speech of the Buddha. But when we become old and infirm and are no longer able to work, no one listens to our words any more. We become the object of humiliation and contempt.

Also, during our youth we think that we will subdue our enemies, support our relatives and work at this and that in order to improve our standard of living and our reputation. Preoccupied with such thoughts, we spend our life not actually fulfilling all our plans. Inevitably, things don't work out exactly as we wanted and we are not able to complete all we had planned, which causes us regret and makes our friends give up hope. In this way we come to the end of our life and there is no time left to make new plans or improve ourselves.

As an example, we can follow the progress of a person in the modern world. He goes to school in his early life and, wanting to gain knowledge, he takes pride in doing well in the examinations. This competitive mind creates a strong determination to improve his mental capacity and talents. His body is at its peak physically at this time and his faculties are acute.

After some time this boy becomes an adult. He looks for a job, falls in love and gets married according to the worldly customs. His adult life begins, he becomes burdened with heavy responsibilities and the free, happy and relaxed times of his youth vanish. Even if he himself is satisfied with his life, he worries about his wife and children and his friends and relatives. He gets caught up in jealousy of his friends who are more successful than him; he is competitive towards his equals and looks down upon those who are inferior. So he experiences multiple sufferings of body and mind, based upon his work, salary and reputation.

At the start, when he has little food and worn clothing, he just wants a job. But when he gets a job, he longs for a better job. He becomes unhappy when he is only given a low salary and is dissatisfied with his status. When his status becomes somewhat higher, he begins to wish for his partner to be inferior to him, and gradually he becomes inflated with pride, thinking that he is better than others. In this fashion, the months and years go by until his life comes to an end.

Thinking back to life in the monasteries in Tibet, there were students who even in their childhood were inclined to learn the scriptures with a mind turned towards understanding the texts well and attaining liberation, which was really excellent. But there were others who studied merely to gain a knowledge greater than that of their fellow students, so that they could create difficulties for their friends during the debating sessions.

Among the more senior lamas and geshes, there were those who occupied their minds totally with the Dharma and abandoned worldly activities as if they were just like waves on the ocean. But some of the Gelugpa geshes may have fallen into the trap of becoming attached to the mere dry name of 'Geshe', thinking, "May I be able to become a Geshe Lharampa," and other thoughts like this. It is extremely difficult for those who seek a good position, such as Abbot of a monastic school for senior geshes or Abbot of a district monastery for junior geshes, to turn their minds to the Dharma. For they spend their lives in a deluded way, acting under the influence of the eight worldly Dharmas. They begin with some disciples and form an association (shaktsang). Gradually they acquire the name of Abbot and many people come to them for divination. People also make offerings, until their material wealth increases to the point where their two hands are not enough to hold it all and they appoint a treasurer. With the treasurer, there are four hands to contain the wealth and when four hands are not enough they appoint an administrator, which makes six hands. They may appoint another person also, which makes eight hands, and so it increases in this way.

34

If one is unable to tame one's inner mind, then being involved in mistaken Dharma practice, which swindles and deceives others, is improper. Even if someone feels he is doing Dharma practice and abiding with a relaxed mind, if he thinks carefully he is just contributing to the eight worldly Dharmas, and it will be difficult to merge his practice with the actual Dharma practice.

If his life passes in this way and he becomes old and infirm, his situation will be like that described by Gungthang Tsang (Je Gungthang Rinpoche): "Twenty years are spent without remembering to practise the holy Dharma, 20 years spent saying, 'I'll do it,' and more than 10 years saying, 'It hasn't happened, it hasn't happened.' This is the story of how one uses up one's life in an empty way."

I have experienced this exactly as it is described here. Before I reached 20 years of age, I was keen to study the texts and had a slight faith in the view of emptiness and bodhicitta. When my mind became more mature, I was forced to think of other things because of having to work on the controversial issue with China. Studying the texts during that difficult period, time passed and I became 25 years old. Then we lost our country and were scattered throughout the world. After that I studied the texts a little, contemplating and practising to some degree and in this way I became 35 or 36 years old.

Then I began to put more energy into my practice, thinking that if one's mind does not merge with actual Dharma practice, one may perform oral recitations for hours upon end without it being true Dharma. At present I am thinking that if I am unable to tame my mind, Dharma will not come. Even with this attitude of placing emphasis on the mind and doing my best to engage in true Dharma practice, still it seems as if the time is approaching when I will have spent 10 years saying, "It hasn't happened, it hasn't happened."

So whether we look decent on the outside or not, if we don't examine our mind properly things become very difficult. We should judge ourselves according to the two main criteria of not having cause for either self-dislike or repentance. If we waste our days and months carelessly, delaying our practice, this is a great loss. Life does not wait: whether we spend our lives meaningfully or not, the time will still be used up moment by moment. So we must do our Dharma practice, for if we let the time go by, saying, "I'll do this and this..." then, as is said here:

Before tomorrow arrives to do Dharma practice,
There's a danger of death arriving today,
So not deceiving your own mind yourself,
If you want to do Dharma practice, do it from today.

For example, I am deceiving myself if I say that I will devote my mind to Dharma practice when I get to be 50 or 60 years old. At present I am in my 30's and I am unable to put effort solely into Dharma. I have other things to think of also, particularly my great responsibility as holder of the name of His Holiness the Dalai Lama. But if I go on making excuses like this I am deceiving myself. Even if it is one day or one hour, if I'm not able to put it into practice without delay then it is my own fault.

Of course, we cannot do the practice of the 84,000 heaps of Dharma all at once. Master and disciple Nagarjuna and Aryadeva, the brothers Asanga and Vasubandhu, the 80 Mahasiddhas and so forth were not able to practise the Dharma completely from the very first day. Initially they had to introduce their minds to Dharma practice. They gradually increased their practices and as they did so their potential for practising Dharma also increased, so that in the end they became indefatigable scholars and practitioners.

They were not born free from defilements, nor endowed with all the good qualities effortlessly. They were like us, as is said in the Bodhicharyavatara ('Guide to the Bodhisattva's Way of Life'), so we should develop the motivation to practise and not feel discouraged. Even meat flies and honey bees possess Buddha nature, so if they could generate the power of enthusiastic perseverance they also would be able to attain enlightenment.

Therefore, since I am born as a human and if I am able to generate the power of enthusiastic perseverance, what is there to stop me from attaining the highest state of enlightenment? We will gain confidence if we understand Buddha nature properly, as it is explained in the 'Paramita'. There is the opportunity to attain the highest state of enlightenment as long as we have the right causes and conditions. It depends on us as individuals whether we choose to use those causes and conditions wisely; if we do, we will definitely attain the highest state of enlightenment. This is the way to generate confidence.

36

If we can bring about a change in our minds, we can convert a certain amount of the actions we have committed from the three doors into virtuous actions, even if not all. Then the opportunity will come to convert small virtuous actions into powerful virtuous actions. Whatever would normally be considered non-virtuous in the general populace may be converted into virtuous actions and become a cause of accumulating extensive merit, by the power of the mind's inner strength. Neutral actions performed by ordinary people can also be converted into virtuous actions if performed by a person of medium capacity. Therefore, gradually changing and improving our minds and practising the Dharma will bear fruits and be the cause of accumulation of merit.

Broadly speaking, the Buddhadharma has two vehicles, known as the Greater and Lesser vehicles. Both sutra and tantra fall within the category of the Greater Vehicle and the Dharma which flourished in the land of Tibet is a combination of both sutra and tantra. In order to practise this type of Dharma one has to understand it. In order to understand it, one has to listen. Therefore, today I shall be continuing with the oral transmission of the Thirty Seven Practices of a Bodhisattva, and you should listen to this teaching by Bodhisattva Thogmed Zangpo with the attitude of one leading all sentient creatures to the highest state of Buddhahood which is free from suffering and its cause, thinking: "There is no other way to help others than by attaining the highest state of enlightenment. May I attain the highest state of enlightenment through practising the path of the Bodhisattvas, completely exhausting all obstacles and becoming endowed with all the good qualities."

I shall continue now with the explanation of how to rely upon the guru. Teachers in general should have these qualities: they should be qualified and knowledgable, good-natured with a great talent for teaching students, and possessed of a sympathetic mind. A spiritual teacher who guides us to the ultimate career must have superior qualities to these, such as the ability to give others right instruction and to be a shining example to follow.

As is said in the Sutra Alankara: "The spiritual teacher should have a tamed, calm and pacified mind, a special knowledge and enthusiasm; he should be rich in the oral transmission with a complete understanding of suchness; he should have a talent for explaining the Dharma, be compassionate by nature and have abandoned disinterest. Seek (such a qualified teacher)."

We require this kind of virtuous spiritual teacher, endowed with 10 qualities, and we should rely upon such a teacher through the nine mental attitudes.[3] Above all, we should create a bond with our lama, forming a closeness between our mind and his. We should listen intently to what he says, and if he is a qualified lama he will lead us to temporary happiness and the path which will benefit us in the future. He will not lead us in the opposite direction, causing our present and future downfall. Likewise, we will receive benefits according to how closely related our mind is with that of our lama.

It is said that it is extremely important for the lama and disciple to analyse each other. The teacher should examine whether it is proper to give teachings to that disciple or not, especially initiations, and whether it is appropriate to speak about tantra. As the disciple, we shouldn't judge our lama according to the opinions of society, such as whether he has a high position or a famous name, is an incarnate lama or an Abbot. Rather, we should examine whether he is suitable to be our guru and whether our faith arises in him or not.

For whether a teacher has a title like Lama, Geshe, Khenpo or Tulku or a long line of previous incarnations—or even the person with the title of Dalai Lama—one should not put one's trust in him just for this reason. It is the talk of Dharma which matters, not society's opinion on the individual's status.

Dharma means to seek nirvana, complete freedom, so the means to approach this free state must be chosen freely. It is incorrect for someone to follow that road under duress. In the 'Lam Rim' Je Rinpoche says, "Have a mind like a good son," which means that disciples should let their minds rely on their guru. A good son does not insist that his opinion is correct; he will do anything his father asks him to do. Likewise, the disciple should act obediently as directed by his or her lama.

The Dharma is validated by reasoning, so whatever we say should be based on reason and not on blind faith and commands. For Dharma disseminated by these unskilful means is forceful but misdirected, like an arrow shot in the dark, and will not survive in

38

the modern world. The Buddhadharma is based on reasoning and possesses a stable foundation, which is why its magnificent rays have spread throughout the world and have not been extinguished.

So, in a nutshell, before committing ourselves to a lama we should analyse carefully; after finding a lama our faith in him should be stable. This is how we should seek our spiritual master.

Now we move onto the subject of taking refuge.

SEVEN

How can a worldly god, himself imprisoned in the jail of
  samsara,
Be able to protect anyone? It is the practice of
Bodhisattvas to go for refuge to the Triple Gem, which
Will never deceive the person who takes refuge in it.

The question is asked, what kind of refuge object is needed? We are bound in the prison of cyclic existence and overpowered by karmic delusions. If we look at worldly kings, demi-gods, local gods or spirits, we will find many tales of the sufferings they inflict upon human beings. If they act positively they can benefit us a little, but not significantly. If they are the kind of beings to whom humans feel they must make live animal sacrifices in order to avoid incurring their wrath, then they are not worthy objects of refuge.

These gods and ghosts are similar to us in that they are overpowered by karma and other defilements. They lack the gross form of a body but resemble us in other respects. They are servants of the same three afflictions as us, namely attachment, hatred and ignorance. So it makes no sense to go for refuge to gods, demi-gods and other beings who are subject to our same afflictions.

We go for refuge looking for fulfilment of our expectations. Which objects of refuge will never deceive us? There are three: the rare and supreme Buddha, Dharma and Sangha. To go for refuge from the very depths of our heart to the Triple Gem, appreciating it as the source of refuge through reasoning, is known as the practice of the Bodhisattvas.

That which is called refuge is what makes the distinction between Buddhist and non-Buddhist. We become Buddhists when we trust in the depths of our heart that the Triple Gem is the true source of refuge; whereas those who lack trust in the Triple Gem and do not accept it as the proper source of refuge are not necessarily Buddhists, even if they know many things about the Buddhadharma.

What is the nature of the Triple Gem—the Buddha, Dharma and Sangha? Buddha means one who is completely free from all faults, having destroyed them. The faults to be destroyed are not external but internal, and broadly speaking we can say that all faults contained in the environment and migratory beings arise through the power of karma. This karma comes from the untamed mind and afflictions. These afflictions constitute any kind of thought which, when it arises, disturbs our mind and interferes with our inner peace. Therefore, to possess afflictions is to suffer. The afflictions gain their name as a result of their mode of action.

Afflictions constitute both attachment and aversion, and the root of them all is ignorance allied with closed-mindedness. Through the power of such afflictions karma accumulates, and through the power of ripened karma sufferings are experienced. The principal afflictions which need to be destroyed are attachment, hatred and ignorance, as well as other mental negativities, including obscurations which prevent us from seeing the subtle nature of phenomena. Our minds become omniscient by overcoming all these hindrances. A person who is endowed with such qualities of mind is known as an Arya Buddha.

Even Buddha is neither permanent nor inherently existent. Nor do Buddhists believe that the Buddha was primordially enlightened, and that we sentient beings must remain forever in our current state. He who manifested the deeds of enlightenment at Bodh Gaya was an ordinary being like us in the beginning. He became a Buddha by abandoning the faults and generating good qualities, step by step. Therefore we also do not have to stay forever as sentient beings in samsara if we follow his example.

It is commonly believed in the world and within the Hinayana view that Buddha was a Bodhisattva in his early life and attained enlightenment while sitting under the Bodhi tree in Bodh Gaya. The Mahayana viewpoint is that all Buddhas never waver from the

40

Dharmakaya and manifest different emanations which appear continuously, either gradually or suddenly, in the pure and impure realms. Among these manifestations was the fourth Buddha, Shakyamuni, who appeared in our world.

He was born as a prince in a royal family, was groomed to rule but then took robes and became a monk. For six years he practised asceticism. Then he overcame Mara and attained enlightenment. That he was enlightened for the first time and had completely destroyed the defilements of dualistic delusion was simply a manifestation.

The Buddha has the nature of the three kinds of body. Dharmakaya is the mind which views the two truths simultaneously and also is endowed with two purities.[4] The body which is endowed with Dharmakaya is the subtle body and only appears to followers who are Arya beings. The full enjoyment body, which is endowed with the five certainties,[5] remains until cyclic existence empties. Such supreme emanation bodies as Shakyamuni Buddha and Kashyapa Buddha appear from this full enjoyment body.

The actual Dharma has two aspects: the quality of abandonment, which in the supreme and precious Dharma includes everything from uprooting any false aspect of the mind to the truth of cessation, which is the complete eradication of the two obscurations[6] in the mind of the Buddha. Then there is the quality of realisation, which means understanding emptiness directly, the truth of the path. Those who are able to generate such qualities of realisation and abandonment become free from every single source of fear, and so the Dharma can be seen as the true protector.

The Sangha comprises those who are endowed with the knowledge of abandonment and realisation. Thus, the supreme Buddha, Dharma and Sangha are the objects of refuge for Buddhists. As proven protectors, the Buddha, Dharma and Sangha are at present separate from us and are the objects of our trust. Like a criminal trusting in his defence lawyer, our minds should seek the protection of these three by going for refuge.

What is involved in the process of seeking protection from the Triple Gem? Dispelling our faults and developing good qualities enable us to be free from suffering and to be endowed with

41

happiness. To achieve this, we must stop accumulating bad karma and create only good karma. In order to do that, we have to destroy the untamed delusional mind which interferes with the accumulation of good karma and the cessation of the development of bad karma.

The basis for dispelling all faults and generating the good qualities is the mind. The mind has many aspects including the five consciousnesses of eye, ear, nose, tongue and body to apprehend their own objects of form, sound, smell, taste and touch. The point where the apprehension of the objects meets is the main consciousness, which is known as mental consciousness. That mental consciousness has different aspects, one of which is functioning while we are awake. There is a more subtle type than this which functions during sleep and when we faint.

At the time of death the gross mental consciousness gradually dissolves and we experience a more subtle consciousness, which by its very nature has never had contact with any afflictions. The afflictions exist within the gross consciousness only, and not in this most subtle consciousness. Therefore, the nature of the mind is free from afflictions. It is when the gross mental consciousness arises that attachment, hatred and so forth manifest from time to time. But these do not affect the nature of the mind.

For example, even if a person is very short-tempered his mind will not always be filled with anger. If the nature of mind was not free from anger, he would experience anger continuously for as long as his mind existed. Also, if afflictions were inseparable from the mind, then the mind could not be shaped or retrained. We seek to abandon the afflictions of the mind but not the mind itself.

Being attached to one object and being repelled by another are two completely different states of mind and cannot exist at the same time. The afflictions such as attachment and aversion arise through ignorance which sees phenomena as truly existent, whereas actually they are not. This is a mistaken thought. There are also positive aspects of the mind, which act as an antidote to these manifestations of ignorance in the mind.

No matter how powerful or strong the afflicted mind is, if we search for it and analyse well we find that whatever it shows us is founded on a lie and is like a bubble which suddenly bursts. We

42

believe that phenomena truly exist but, if they really do, we should be able to prove their true existence when we investigate them. Instead, our investigation reveals that they don't truly exist in their own right. Once we have discovered this, it is not possible for belief in the true existence of phenomena to arise.

Following this reasoning, the temporary faulty mind has no stable base because it is founded on ignorance, whereas the good aspect of the mind has a valid support. The faulty, deluded mind exists in a state of degeneration and, if we familiarise ourselves with the positive aspects of mind which have valid support, it is certain that this deluded mind will become weaker and weaker. It is like the heat of a fire which, as it becomes hotter and hotter, causes the cold to be reduced; or like the light which dispels the darkness more and more thoroughly as it becomes more and more powerful.

So when the positive qualities of the mind are developed, the faulty aspects lose power and eventually disappear. But if during practice the potential of the good qualities of mind were to decrease, the negative aspect would once again increase. For instance, if someone who trains in bodhicitta continuously for several months sees some improvement but then neglects his contemplation on bodhicitta for a while, he will cease to see any improvement. This is because he doesn't have the stable and valid support of the wisdom which realises emptiness.

The support becomes firmer if we practise with the combination of method and wisdom, and as a result the wholesome mind becomes stable and powerful. Because all these qualities are dependent upon the mind, they increase immeasurably when we practise and train in this manner continuously; in this way we are sure to increase our good qualities and reduce our faults. This achievement of good qualities and reduction in the deluded qualities of the mind is known as Buddhahood. Ultimately, we have to generate the truth of the path in our mental continuum. This is the supreme Dharma. As a result, we attain the qualities of cessation of every single affliction of the mind. Then we will be free from suffering and will enjoy indestructible pleasure.

We should practise gradually in this way. Otherwise, simply being aware as we are at present of the separate entity of the Triple

43

Gem does not pacify our suffering. In our current state it is difficult to attain the qualified supreme Dharma.[7] However, we should try to attain this state of qualified supreme Dharma by gradually undertaking the preliminary practices before entering into the path.

The main gateway on the path of discarding faults and gaining good qualities is the practice of abandoning the 10 non-virtuous actions. Of these, the three non-virtuous or unwholesome deeds of the body are killing, stealing and sexual misconduct. Killing any living creature, from human beings down to minor insects, should be avoided. If we kill, this action harms the body and life of another and thus causes it to experience the torment of suffering. This is why it is said that killing involves us in extremely heavy negativity. Such an action is either motivated by anger, as in killing our enemy, or by attachment, as in killing animals to eat their meat.

Some Mahayana Buddhist texts state that it is alright to eat meat, whereas others state it is not alright. In the Vinaya, or discipline texts, it is said that certain kinds of meat are forbidden, but meat eating in itself is not completely disallowed. In common practice, it is considered alright to eat meat bought from the market and which is considered to be pure in three aspects, rather than eating the meat of an animal we have specifically ordered to be killed for this purpose. This topic is covered in the 'Essence of Madhyamika', among other texts.

The fact that some people have completely forsworn the eating of meat is excellent. However, if giving up meat adversely affects our health and threatens our very survival while practising the Dharma, then we have to weigh up which is the more important and judge each individual case. The killing of animals specifically for their meat is an unskilful action which makes us feel sad. What is more, there is the terrible custom of killing animals for offerings, motivated by ignorance. It would be wonderful if there was no one in this gathering who performs such animal sacrifices in his or her culture. But if there are some here who follow this custom, then when you go back home you should tell your people that His Holiness the Dalai Lama forbids animal sacrifices. If by saying this you are able to call a halt to such practices in your community, that is very good.

If you have some gods who need animal flesh as offerings, tell them that although you have the intention to make these offerings to

44

them, you have been asked by His Holiness the Dalai Lama not to do so and so you are helpless. In this way, you can lay the blame on me. Although I have no power nor any kind of realisation, I am saying this while seeking refuge in the texts of Lord Buddha, and so it is a reasonable statement to make. If some of you here are in the habit of making such animal sacrifices yourselves, now that you have received the Kalacakra initiation you must stop this practice at once. This is like a sacred connection or commitment, based on these spiritual discourses.

Those to whom people sacrifice animal flesh are like demons, who have a strong craving for flesh and blood. They are not worthy of offerings because they have no power in themselves to take the lives of others, so they seek an occasion to eat such food reliant upon mankind.

The next non-virtuous action to be abandoned is stealing, or taking things which are not given, and this includes anything from a precious ornament right down to the smallest miscellaneous item. Stealing trespasses upon the possessions of others. Although it does not inflict the same amount of harm as taking life, nevertheless the person deprived of his or her possessions experiences suffering.

Stealing has many aspects: for instance, we may find and then keep a possession which someone else has lost. Even though we have not directly stolen it, nevertheless its owner has not mentally given up that object. So there is a chance that we will accrue negativities similar to those we would earn by actually stealing it. According to the Dharma view, if we find an object belonging to someone else we should search for the owner and return it to him or her.

There are various kinds of sexual misconduct. In lay people's terms sexual misconduct generally refers to having sexual intercourse with others apart from one's spouse. This is a principal source of quarrels and conflicts among all people from the minister of a developed country to the barbarians in an undeveloped land. So such conflicts will not occur if people abandon this type of sexual misconduct.

Next, we come to unwholesome speech which refers to telling lies, malicious and harsh speech and idle gossip. Telling lies means saying we have seen something we haven't seen or, conversely, saying we have not seen something we have in fact seen. This is motivated by the desire to alter other people's views and is extremely unskilful behaviour, because it deceives and cheats others. It is important always to speak the truth.

Malicious speech means talk which disrupts harmonious relationships between people. It is harmful to society as a whole and robs the individual of happiness and ease of mind, so it is very bad. The great lamas of the Kadampa lineage have said: "Be attentive to your speech when you are in a crowd and be attentive to your mind when you are alone. Just by opening your mouth, you may become trapped in the lower realms." This is true. By speaking in a certain manner, we may cause other people to earn censure or blame and there is a danger of accumulating negativities this way, so we should always pay attention to our speech.

Harsh speech refers to saying bad words. When I am talking to others it sometimes seems as if harsh words are about to come out of my mouth, so I also need to be careful of my speech. When anger arises, we should not use harsh speech to others, by saying things like, "You good-for-nothing!" or "You idiot!" Harsh speech afflicts the minds of others and should be abandoned, as should slang and sloppy speech, like, "Hey, you!" and "Hey, man!" when used to belittle others. The previous Dalai Lama, for example, always used to attract someone's attention by calling out their name.

Idle gossip refers to speaking without any purpose and arises out of delusion. Examples include talking about dirty things for the sake of it, or discussing war and conflicts. In brief, we should cease to indulge in gossip or talk which causes an increase in our delusions, such as attachment and anger towards ourselves and others. Say whatever it is necessary to say and at other times remain quiet. That is very good.

Now we can discuss the unwholesome deeds of the mind, which are of three kinds, namely covetousness, ill-will and wrong view. Covetousness refers to focusing upon the material possessions of others and hoping and praying that we may acquire those. Ill-will means to focus on others with an antagonistic mind and an intention to inflict harm. Wrong view includes thinking there is no life after death, no cause and effect nor the Triple Gem, and is considered to carry very heavy negative weight. Recognising these 10 unwholesome

46

deeds and abandoning them is known as the practice of the 10 wholesome deeds.

The entrance to our Dharma practice starts from here. Gradually, having developed our minds, we generate the wish to free ourselves from samsara as well as generating the altruistic intention to help others. Similarly, little by little we can attain the path of truth within ourselves with all its characteristics—seeing the nature of impermanence in objects, the nature of selflessness in phenomena and the nature of suffering in the afflictions of sentient beings. We create happiness and freedom from suffering by depending upon the path of cessation and of truth. Therefore, the Dharma is known by Buddhists as the true refuge.

The precious Sangha is also very important as an example to be followed, and I find it very helpful. Not counting the beings who existed during the Completion Era,[8] we come across people these days also who are less concerned with worldly affairs and are prepared to sacrifice social activities in order to really practise love, compassion and bodhicitta, and the profound and extensive stages of the path right to the very core. When I meet such people, I think to myself, "Why haven't I done as they have done? What is preventing me from doing it? I'll definitely do it." Thoughts such as these arise in our minds owing to the benefits and kindness of spiritual friends, the Sangha. So such people should be considered as objects of emulation and good spiritual friends, whether or not they are a part of the actual precious Sangha. And we should practise the Dharma ourselves, following their example.

According to the Mahayana teachings, those members of the actual precious Sangha have cultivated bodhicitta in their continuum and, supported by bodhicitta, have attained the union of calm abiding and special insight samadhi by realising emptiness directly. Having attained the quality of the first ground and above, they are courageous and able to work successfully for the benefit of others. They have a marvellous inner strength, are endowed with immaculate knowledge and are invincible. So we can see that the Buddha is the protector and is like a doctor, the precious Dharma is the real protection and is like the medicine, and the spiritual Sangha is like a nurse, taking care of us like a good friend.

47

Those Bodhisattvas who are seeking the highest state of enlightenment in order to benefit others are practising the seeking of refuge in the Triple Gem. Taking refuge is the practice of a Bodhisattva, and with this statement the seventh stanza concludes.

EIGHT

It has been said by Muni that the unbearable sufferings
Of the lower realms are the result of negative karma.
Therefore, it is the practice of Bodhisattvas never to create
Negative karma, even at the cost of their lives.

The suffering of the lower migratory beings is extremely hard to bear, such as the hell beings who suffer extreme heat and cold, being boiled, burned and frozen. Then there are the sufferings endured in the other kinds of hell realms, such as the supplementary hell and the realms close to hell.

"Whatever action you perform, a concomitant reaction or result will follow." This may seem inconceivable to our cognising minds, yet knowledge itself is limitless and so we cannot say this is implausible; there are so many things beyond the ordinary person's consciousness. The various kinds of sufferings of the lower realms result from impure actions, "The Buddha said: 'All these arise out of the deluded mind.'" Just as he said so it seems, that different environments and sentient beings of the lower realms manifest out of the deluded mind.

I don't know whether all of these exist based on the measurements given in the Abhidharma Kosha, or the Treasury of Knowledge, but certainly the hell realms do exist. We witness a whole variety of sentient activity even in this mundane human realm, with different aspects of the body, of livelihood and lifestyle, and others exist beyond our imagination. Based on this, we may infer that such conditions exist also in the hundred other worlds of the mundane realms.

Let us consider the sufferings of the hungry ghosts, for example: they mainly suffer from a lack of food and drink. Those devils to whom people perform animal sacrifices belong in this realm. They were born as

48

hungry ghosts because of their accumulated bad karma. Among them are some who have more power than others and they humiliate those in an inferior position; others within this hierarchy are rebellious.

Next we should look at the sufferings of the animals in our world. There are animals such as dogs, horses and mules which we look after, and others like sheep and goats which are raised to be slaughtered. If we think about it we realise that their lives don't belong to them. They have no intention to inflict harm on people; they eat grass, drink water, are dull and ignorant. These are the conditions of their lives. So what gives humans the right to eat their bodies?

When these animals are given a little food, they scramble and fight with each other to get at it, out of attachment and anger. In addition, they must endure the suffering of being beaten with sticks. Looking carefully at all these things leads us to see the sadness of the small potential that these animals have. There is no one ultimately to protect and support them, and they have to search for their own food.

We human beings have established schools in the pursuit of knowledge, hospitals to improve people's health and hygiene, and many factories for the production of goods and to give the workers a livelihood. We also set up farms and cater to the nomadic way of life. Yet veterinary hospitals, which are meant for animals, mainly serve the purpose of humans who use the animals to provide them with a livelihood. Such places are not established out of feelings of pity and compassion for the animals themselves.

We humans discuss our worries and our problems, such as lacking an opportunity for study, or not getting good medicines or admission to a good hospital. But if one is born in animal form, to whom is one going to complain about all these problems? For instance, if a sheep, goat or hen is run over by a car, no one carries it to the hospital because it has broken its leg. In fact, someone may even kill it. So animals have no supporters or protectors. Would we be able to bear it if we were born as a dog or a pig, without protection or support, without relatives to look after us?

Circumstances are extremely difficult for beings in the hell realms and the realms of the hungry ghosts, as they are also for animals. At present we have attained a human birth, but we have no choice as to whether we will be born in the hell, hungry ghost or animal realms in our next life. We have to go wherever our karma leads us.

If we have strong virtuous actions, impeccably accumulated, then we may have the confidence of knowing that we will not take birth in the lower realms. Otherwise it is easy to end up in the lower realms, unless we have the opportunity to confess our accumulated negative deeds and make a firm commitment within the framework of the four powers [9] not to commit such unwholesome actions again.

Aryadeva comments:

> The majority of people follow
> The way of unholy beings, and so
> Most ordinary beings definitely
> Descend to the lower migrations.

It follows, therefore, that the majority of people coming here for the Kalacakra initiation will descend to the lower migrations. Since it is difficult to attain a good rebirth, those who do not practise the Dharma will most probably go down to the lower realms. If you descend to that lower migratory state, will you be able to bear the suffering? And do you have the confidence now that you will not be reborn in the lower realms? If not, you must be cautious and practise without delay.

Seek refuge in the Buddha, Dharma and Sangha by understanding their real qualities. In order to become the Buddha, Dharma and Sangha yourself, you must abandon the 10 non-virtuous deeds, with a concomitant strong faith in the law of cause and effect. Based on this, recite the six-syllable mantra as often as possible, do prostrations and circumambulation. Train as much as you can in renunciation and bodhicitta and gradually try to improve your mental continuum. At the very least, you should train yourself to abandon the 10 unwholesome deeds, and in addition you should do prostrations and circumambulate. The Buddha, who always spoke the truth, said that the result of negative action is immeasurable suffering. If you know this by the power of your reasoning, you will not engage in negative actions even at the cost of your life. This is the practice of a Bodhisattva.

50

So far we have been discussing the person of small scope. Next we shall consider the common path and the person of middle scope.

NINE

The happiness of the three worlds, like dewdrops on the
tip of a
Blade of grass, has the nature of vanishing in a moment.
Therefore, it is the practice of Bodhisattvas to strive
For the excellent state of changeless liberation.

The pleasures and good qualities of this cyclic existence—which is included in the three conditional existences[10]—can be compared to drops of dew on the tip of a blade of grass. One moment there is a shining dewdrop, the next moment it dissolves without trace. Likewise, all the happiness and pleasure of the three conditional existences have no stable base and are characterised by uncertainty; it is their nature to perish in a moment. Nirvana is an unchangeable state of eternal happiness, and the seeking of nirvana is the practice of a Bodhisattva.

It is not only that the three lower migrations contain great suffering. If we think carefully, we can see that there is never any happiness until we become completely free from cyclic existence. Currently we have attained a human birth, which is the most excellent form in cyclic existence. But let us look at this present condition. Being uncertain of the place of our rebirth, we experience constant anxiety. Our present temporary freedom from the lower migrations holds no stability, and there will be none until we can be confident of becoming totally free from cyclic existence. This is the way things are.

Through investigation we can see that the nature of this human body is suffering. Perhaps it can be said that there are no strong feelings of pleasure and suffering for the first few weeks of life, immediately after conception. But then the foetus starts to feel happiness and pain acutely. When it moves in the womb, it does so not from pleasure but out of a sense of discomfort, because it is impossible to remain calm and relaxed while confined in the womb. And it must remain there for about nine or 10 months, not merely a few days or weeks. After taking birth, the baby goes through a period of experiencing suffering like an insect does, for although it has a human form it can't act freely. In this way life begins with suffering.

In the interim, between the ages of 15 or 16 and 40 to 50 years of age, women are considered to be attractive and men to be handsome and strong. At this stage of life we think that we are able to shoulder anything, without needing to rely on or seek support from anyone else because we can use our own talents. Yet, as I mentioned earlier, there is always some sense of unsatisfactoriness in our lives.

We may go into business and find that it doesn't go well; or we go to school but cannot study properly and receive poor marks in our examinations; we may look for a job but get poorly paid; a young man may marry a girl and find she is unable to bear children, bringing the suffering of not having children; they approach lamas, asking them to pray for children to be conceived. Or there is the couple with many children, who worry about whether they should use birth control and, if they do use it, whether it accords with the law of cause and effect. If they don't use birth control, how will they manage to care for all their children? Thinking along these lines also causes suffering.

Then if we have no money, what are we to do? If we eat such-and-such a food this year, what shall we eat next year? If we are satisfied and have enough for our own needs, we think about what we can give to our relatives. We may think it is good to lend money, but if we do, would we get good interest or not? Keeping the money in the bank doesn't yield much interest, so we may decide to lend money to a business person. Then we worry about finding a trustworthy person, and we ask for divination and say prayers for that. All of this means that we become a slave to our money instead of reaping benefit from it.

A man who has no wife suffers because of that. If he has a wife, he worries that she is not beautiful and modest. If she is beautiful as well as modest, he worries about being able to support her adequately. We suffer if we have no relatives or friends, thinking that we have no one to guide us and show us the path; we are alone. We also suffer if we have friends and relatives but we don't get along with them.

Then, at the other end of life, we become old and infirm and

52

experience suffering as a result. And life ends with death, which itself has the nature of suffering. The anticipation of death gives rise to fear and anxiety, so most people ask lamas to pray for their long life and freedom from disease. But even if they try to prevent sickness by eating only moderate amounts of food and maintaining very good hygiene, the suffering of death will still befall them despite these precautions.

The suffering known as death comes about either from exhausting our karma or our merit, or owing to negative conditions. The day comes when we lie in bed, using our body for the last time. Although we may be used to having a healthy and supple body, on that day we fall over like an old tree and are unable to roll over in our beds without assistance. When we lie on our side, we experience suffering in the form of pain, and if we are in hospital we must rely upon the nurses to turn us from side to side.

If we need to have an operation shortly before we die, parts of our body will be cut open and we may even have new parts or substances inserted. If it is necessary for our survival to perform surgery on our hands, they will do so; if they need to amputate one of our feet, that will be done; and if it is necessary to perform surgery on our heart then they will do that also.

Everyone around us will be busy tending to our needs on that final day while we lie there thinking, "Now I am about to die," and experiencing grief. The way in which we have spent the past 50 or 60 years comes to seem like last night's dream. We face permanent separation in this life from our near and dear relatives and friends. We have to die and go on to the next life, while they must remain in this human world. So because of this fact we weep and wear an expression of great sadness, and our relatives' and friends' eyes also fill with tears. Murmuring forlorn words, we must go our separate ways.

Although we Tibetan people have been separated from each other, there is at least the possibility of meeting up again; whereas the separation caused by death is not a result of one country exploiting another but of finishing our karma. We cannot strike a bargain with anyone to let us stay by using any method such as bribery or our native cunning.

Some of my disciples may be prepared to sacrifice their lives for me out of their strong faith in the Dharma. Yet when the day comes for me to die, I must go alone. I cannot take anyone with me, saying, "He is my friend," or, "He is my attendant," or that he is a person whom His Holiness the Dalai Lama trusts. My disciples have to stay behind, and all of you must also stay. As it is said: "A king has to leave this world, forsaking his kingdom; a beggar has to leave this world, forsaking his stick."

We are tormented by intense suffering as we speak our last words in our deathbed speech on that final day, and it costs us an effort to speak at all. We may have great difficulty in making ourselves understood because of the dryness of our mouths and, if so, our relatives and friends become griefstricken, helpless and depressed.

Before this time we were used to expressing ourselves freely. As a small example, we would complain out loud if the mo-mo we were eating were not properly cooked. We would definitely speak up if they were too hot and burnt our mouths. We would scold the person responsible if we were in a position of authority, and would curse him behind his back if we could not challenge him to his face. We have been used to feeling in control in this way, but at the time of death we can't even eat.

Here is another example: many Tibetans wear amulets, which they say contain the relics of such-and-such and the flesh of such-and-such Buddha or Bodhisattva. For this reason they are reluctant to hand them to anyone else but wear them always around their necks. On that final day, others will open the amulet and mix the contents with water, and then those holy substances and relics are put into the dying person's mouth as the last meal. But often the person doesn't even have the strength to sip, so those substances remain inside his or her mouth even when he or she is dead.

At the time of death the sound of our breathing slowly alters, like the breaking of a violin string, and whatever pleasurable feelings we experienced in our life come to an end with our last, unusually forceful, out-breath, after which all breath ceases.

All the methods we may have used in the hospital to try to survive will be of no benefit when our karma is exhausted. It will not help even if the surgeon has given us a new heart or a new set of lungs, or if we are given oxygen to aid our breathing. We are completely helpless. At that stage:

54

The doctor gives up on us and prayers won't overcome
    our obstacles;
Our relatives lose hope of our survival. We feel helpless
    and don't know what to do.
That is the time for the precious guru,
Arya Avalokiteshvara, to protect us and lead us from
    cyclic existence.

As is said here in 'Compassionate Protection', at the time of
death it is the deity to whom we give our devotion and the energy
with which we have practised the Dharma which make our minds
happy and relaxed. They will give us confidence and consolation.
Nothing esle will help us because there is no other protector or
supporter.

To summarise what I have just been saying, we experience
suffering when we are young and healthy as well as when we become
old and infirm. We suffer when our lifestyle improves as well as when
we face reduced circumstances. We are overpowered by different kinds
of suffering from the beginning of life until the moment of death.

So what is the purpose of a human rebirth? If we become a slave
to wealth and possessions and the mere caretaker of our house, it is
meaningless. A house is actually meant to offer people shelter, so it is
good if we can feel comfortable and relaxed in our home. But if we
are too busy taking care of it, we become its servant or caretaker.
Similarly, wealth and possessions should benefit people, but if we
don't know how to use them properly we become their slave.

Although it seems like a dirty subject to discuss, the main purpose
of food and clothing really seems to be to produce excrement. Food is
the actual source of excrement, and normal excrement is formed by
taking in moderate amounts of food and wearing appropriate clothing.

However, choosing to train our minds in the Dharma gives
meaning to remaining in human existence because we become calm
and relaxed temporarily and also receive benefit in the long run. We
should not say that this life has no essence. If we say that life is
meaningless and we commit suicide, we must take another birth,
however unwillingly; for ending this life does not mean that we will
cease taking birth. Being reborn is not a matter of wanting to or not
wanting to—we must continue taking birth until we can exhaust our

actions and afflicted thoughts. So unless we are able to abandon the root cause of rebirth, it is useless. We will never find permanent happiness and ease as long as we continue to take birth, but will instead spend our lives in suffering.

What is it that causes all this suffering? It is the aggregates we have taken on, created by action and delusion. Why have we taken this birth? Not only because of our father and mother, but because of our accumulated actions. We can stop this cycle of rebirth by investigating and uprooting the continuity of actions. It is necessary to exhaust the store of our actions in order to cease taking birth, and to exhaust our accumulated actions we must exhaust our afflictions. On the day that we manage to exhaust our actions and our afflictions, we attain liberation.

In other words, once we have exhausted the afflictions which create karma and completely exhausted our very disposition to grasp at true existence, and once we have attained the cessation of every affliction and action, then we attain nirvana. Thus Dharmadhatu, which is obtained as a result of exhausting actions and afflictions, is known as liberation as well as cessation.

After attaining liberation, the conventional 'I' of the person continues to exist. It doesn't mean that we vanish completely, although it is true that we are not forced to take birth again propelled by our karma and delusions. There are misinterpretations in many Western books about Buddhism, where it is written that when a person attains nirvana he or she ceases to exist. This is not the case. We gain actual freedom by attaining nirvana and we don't have to rely on anyone, although this does not refer to external things.[11] We must explore our ability to attain nirvana through practice if we are to reach such a state of being.

Anger and attachment arise based on our very root tendency to grasp at inherent existence. In the Madhyamikavatara ('Guide to the Middle Way') it says that:

First clinging to the self as 'I', then clinging to possessions as 'mine', migratory beings become trapped in cyclic existence, like a treadmill going round and round without freedom. Prostrate to compassion itself.

56

Practioners perceive through their wisdom that all the
drawbacks of afflictions arise from the perception of this
transitory collection of aggregates as 'I' and 'mine'; they
see that they themselves are merely a transitory collection
of aggregates, and thus refute the concrete existence if 'I'.

We begin with this tendency to think of 'I', and from that we
conclude that this 'I' is completely different from others. Based on
this, there arises the sense of 'my relatives' and 'my possessions' and
then anger arises out of such thought processes. We should explore the
root of all these false notions, seeing how 'I' appears in our mind, how
our mind apprehends the 'I' and whether it truly exists as appre-
hended. We have to investigate the connection between these notions,
by using our reasoning as explained in the Madhyamika text:

It arises not from self nor from other;
Not from both of these, nor from no cause.
Whatever the object may be,
It has never been born in any place.

As it says in the root text, we have to investigate to see whether
there is a connection between how we apprehend phenomena and
how they exist, how they appear to our minds and how our minds
crave them. We will definitely get a glimpse of the nature of reality if
we determine the truth to some degree by such investigation, and
from that we can gain trust in achieving liberation in the future.

However important and precious one person is, he or she is only
one, one alone; whereas other sentient beings are infinite and limitless
in number, and share our desire to be happy and avoid suffering. We
all deserve and possess the same right to eliminate suffering from our
lives and to accomplish happiness, and we have the same potential for
this. So if we compare the importance of ourselves and others, we can see
that others are extremely important.

I have attained a human body and, among human beings, I am a
person who believes in the Dharma, I am a Dharma practitioner.
Within that category, I am a Mahayana Dharma practitioner. My
status is that of a fully ordained monk who has taken the Bodhisattva
vow as well as the vow of tantra. I can therefore say that I am an upholder

57

of wisdom and the triple vow. So I have attained a comparatively precious and important status.

Yet if I compare myself with other sentient beings, I am infinitesimally small in importance compared to them. I am only one person who feels either happiness or suffering and I will still only be one person if I wander in this cyclic existence from beginningless time until far into the future. So what would be so special about me attaining liberation right now? But if I am able to benefit others and give them even a small amount of pleasure, that is worth something. The benefit truly extends outwards to an infinite number of beings.

Just as we may sacrifice temporary happiness for the sake of attaining the supreme bliss of nirvana, so may we choose to make the worthy sacrifice of our own happiness in order to be of benefit to others. It is considered normal to forego the small things of this world in order to attain something greater. Similarly, the wise person sacrifices himself or herself in order to benefit others.

TEN

What is the use of our own happiness when all mothers
who have been
Kind to us since beginningless time are suffering?
Therefore, it is the practice of Bodhisattvas to generate
Bodhicitta in order to liberate all sentient beings.

We have to generate the aspiration to seek supreme and complete Buddhahood in order to free limitless numbers of sentient beings from suffering and its cause. We should generate this intention if it has not already been generated, and increase it if it has already been generated. This is the practice of a Bodhisattva.

From here onwards in the text, the actual practice of bodhicitta is dealt with. To learn the reason why we have to exchange self for others, we should read on:

ELEVEN

As all sufferings are born out of desiring one's own
  happiness,
And the Buddhas are born out of the mind which ben-
  efits others,
It is the practice of Bodhisattvas to engage in the actual
Exchange of their happiness for the sufferings of others.

In the Bodhicharyavatara ('Guide to the Bodhisattva's Way of
Life') it is written:

All the sufferings in the world
Arise out of wanting happiness for self;
All the happiness in the world
Arises out of wanting happiness for others.

and:

What else is there to say? So many things.
Ordinary people act to benefit themselves,
While Mahamuni works for others.
Look at the difference between these two.

The root of all happiness lies in wanting others to be happy. The
source of all obstacles lies in wanting happiness for oneself alone. As
also stated in the 'Gurupuja':

All gates to weakness are due to self-cherishing.
All the bases of positive qualities are
Due to cherishing one's mothers.

The condition we are in at present is a result of cherishing ourselves
fiercely and forsaking others. Now we are following the fourth Buddha,
Shakyamuni, and have met the Mahayana teachings. Most particularly,
we have been introduced to the path of exchanging self for others,
transmitted by the Acharya Arya Nagarjuna, based on the instructions
given by Manjushri as well as from the lineage of Shantideva.

So, right now, we should look at the obstacles from every angle
and abandon our self-cherishing attitude. We should look at the
qualities of cherishing others from every angle and practise as much

as possible to train our mind in exchanging self for others. In order to increase our motivation to exchange self for others in the form of practice,

> Train to give and take alternately;
> The sequence of taking should begin from the self.
> Mount them both upon your breath.

The reference to this practice is from the Bodhicharyavatara ('Guide to the Bodhisattva's Way of Life'): "One should practise that holy secret." It is said that we should contemplate the unwanted sufferings of sentient beings and should wish, verbally and emotionally, to take on their sufferings out of compassion.

Sentient beings lack happiness at present, much though they desire it, so we should train our mind in offering our body, possessions and all our wholesome deeds of the three doors—in fact, whatever we have—with love to sentient beings who are infirm and lacking in happiness. This is what is known as tong-len practice. In the 'Gurupuja' it is stated:

> Compassionate lama, may all the sufferings,
> Obscurations and negativities of mother-like
> Sentient beings be ripened on to me completely.
> By giving my happiness and wholesome deeds to others,
> May all sentient beings be blessed with happiness.

And it says in the 'Precious Garland':

> May I be ripened by their suffering.
> May my wholesome deeds be ripened upon them.

We have to train in this way and should therefore study the following lines:

> It is the practice of the Bodhisattvas to engage in the
> actual exchange of their happiness for the sufferings of
> others.

We gain not only ultimate happiness but also happiness in the short-term through training in bodhicitta and practising exchanging self for others. Whereas if we persist in having a self-cherishing

60

attitude and do not practise exchanging self for others, we will not gain any temporary happiness, let alone attaining nirvana and the omniscient state. In order to demonstrate this truth, it is said that:

> If one does not exchange one's happiness
> For the sufferings of others, one will
> Not become enlightened and will experience no
> Happiness even in this cyclic existence.

DAY THREE

Introductory Talk

Looking back on our lives, we can see that whatever meaningful things we have done are profitable. But if we have spent our life in a way that we now regret, whatever time has gone is beyond reach. We cannot ask Time to move slowly for us, because when a period of time has finished, it has finished. Time won't wait.

When we make a mistake in our work we can say that we want the opportunity to try again; whereas if we consider that we've spent our life in an empty and meaningless way, there's no point in saying, "Please may I start again?" because there is no way to make that happen. We spent some of our childhood years in a meaningless way because we were not able to think properly, but our understanding increased as we grew older. We knew things and we could think and we listened to the teachings. It seems we knowingly misused our time if we then continued to spend our lives meaninglessly.

If this is the case, the only thing we can do is confess our past misdeeds, focusing on the negative karma accumulated, and try to purify it by circumambulating, making offerings, reciting mantras, erecting images of body, speech and mind, taking vows, and meditating on emptiness and bodhicitta. Meditating on emptiness and bodhicitta are supreme among these. We can also benefit from doing 100,000 prostrations related to the purification of negativities, offering 100,000 mandalas, and reciting the 100-syllable mantra related to the Vajrasattva meditation 100,000 times. These are the practices we should use when making our confession, deliberately focusing on the negativities of our early life.

We shouldn't just say that we have committed such-and-such a negative action, but should make an assessment of all our misdeeds, recollecting their details and then contemplating them with the thought, "It is really bad that I have done such things which are against the teachings of the Buddha and the wishes of my guru. They will lead to my ruin in this life as well as ultimate ruin. They are against the holy Dharma and are also not socially acceptable."

62

Then we should think, "I have obtained the leisure and beneficial circumstances of a human birth and I have met the Dharma and a spiritual friend. But despite this I have not done the things I should have done, and I have done things I shouldn't have done, which will cause suffering for myself and others. I have acted like a man who can see yet falls off a cliff, or like someone deliberately eating poison. From today onwards, I shall never again commit such bad actions, even at the cost of my life." The compassionate and skilful Buddha said that our negativities can be purified if we confess our past misdeeds with a strong sense of regret. So we should confess and make a proper commitment in reliance on the four powers.

The first of the four powers is taking refuge and mind generation, the power of basis. The second is the power of regret, in which the repentance we feel for the negativities accumulated in our earlier life is as strong as if we had swallowed poison. We should recite mantras as part of the third power—engaging in the practice of applying antidotes—in order to make a confession of our negativities. Finally, there is the power of promise, that in future we will never again commit such bad actions even at the cost of our life.

Before commencing this practice, first we should sincerely take refuge and practise mind generation. Then we count every negativity we have accumulated in the past on the beads of our mala and think of them in terms of the negativities accumulated based on our body, speech and mind. We should also think of the negativities arising from natural misdeeds and misdeeds caused by neglecting discipline.

Those who have taken vows should repent, thinking, "I have taken the vows of a novice, or a fully ordained monk, and the vows of bodhicitta and tantra, and yet the way I have spent my life is like ordinary people of low status who have taken no vows and do not practise the Dharma. So I really am a wretched, flawed person." It is important to confess our misdeeds with thoughts such as these and make a strong commitment.

If someone should ask whether it is possible to purify negativities by making such a confession the answer is, as Milarepa said, that the negativities will be purified if the repentance is sincere. True repentance for our past misdeeds will enable us to generate the strength of mind not to commit such negativities in the future. However, if we lack such true repentance and merely pretend to generate a commitment not to repeat such negative actions even at the cost of our life, this is just a fabrication and the strength of mind cannot develop. So it is most important to develop true repentance, and in order to do that we should contemplate the disadvantages of such negativities. We need to think about the law of cause and effect, or karma, to really appreciate the disadvantages, because we may not discover the results of negative actions if we are not convinced of the law of cause and effect.

We should follow this process and then make a firm commitment, thinking, "I shall make every day meaningful from today onwards, and not spend my time in an empty way. The only proper way is to spend my life doing good, being well-behaved and courteous and transgressing neither the Dharma nor the wishes of the enlightened beings. However many lives I have still to live, I shall definitely spend them in a meaningful way." We should listen to the Dharma with this intention as well as with the attitude of completely accomplishing the purpose of self and others.

Now I shall briefly summarise the holy teachings of the Thirty Seven Practices of a Bodhisattva which we have discussed so far. First is the combination of the three practices of listening, contemplating and meditating on the profound and extensive baskets of Mahayana (moral discipline, discourses and knowledge) by the Bodhisattvas. After that we need to practise the meaning of the Dharma which we have heard, and for that we should stay in a place far away from attachment and anger. Thus, abandoning one's fatherland is the second practice of a Bodhisattva. But simply staying away from our fatherland is nothing fantastic in itself; we should seek a solitary place, this being the third practice of a Bodhisattva. The fourth practice of a Bodhisattva is to abandon worldly life, for we will not benefit if our mind remains under the influence of the eight worldly Dharmas even while staying in a solitary place.

We need good friends and a qualified spiritual guru in order to maximise the potential for practice, so the fifth practice of a Bodhisattva is to forsake evil friends. The sixth practice of a Bodhisattva is to depend on our teacher in a correct way, both with the right attitude as well as with our material goods.

64

From here onwards, the first entrance is taking refuge in order to engage in the real practice. To do this, we must recognise these three—the precious Buddha, Dharma and Sangha—as the indisputable protectors for all Buddhists. We must have trust and faith in the Triple Gem as a distinct entity separate from ourselves, and we should reflect that whatever things happen to us, be they good or bad, only the Triple Gem can save us. We should go for refuge in this way and with the idea of gaining the precious Buddha, Dharma and Sangha within.

It is not enough simply to take refuge; we should practise according to the advice related to taking refuge, which includes refraining from such improper activities as making prostrations and offerings to non-human beings using techniques not taught in the Buddhist teachings, belittling the body, mind and speech of Buddha, or looking upon holy images as possessions and holding on to them for financial surety.

Nowadays some people trade in images and spiritual texts. These traders will reap heavy penalties in terms of negativities and obstacles if the images and texts they are selling belonged to people who believe in and practise the Dharma. Buying and selling antique images of Buddha and ritual objects for a great deal of money may increase their material possessions, but actually their acts are the same as eating poison.

It is a different case if someone, with a resolute intention to preserve the continuity of the teachings through printing rare texts, takes out a loan for the printing and sells the texts for enough money to cover costs and to print some more texts. This is money borrowed and spent in pursuit of wholesome work. But those who sell texts and claim to be serving the Dharma, whereas in reality they are serving their stomachs, are involved in dangerous activity—so be sure not to do such things. I shouldn't fail to mention such examples when they occur in the text, because they have a purpose. But whether or not an individual is able to practise according to this advice depends upon him or her.

It is important not to deliberately belittle the Triple Gem. We may rely upon powerful gods and spirits as our friends, for temporary benefit, in the process of going for refuge to the Buddha. But it is

65

incorrect to regard those spirits as our lamas and our deities, so we should avoid this behaviour.

Likewise, going for refuge to the Dharma means that we must not inflict harm upon sentient beings. We should also take care not to treat the texts disrespectfully. For example, it is improper to keep the text which reveals the meaning of the Tripitaka or the Three Higher Trainings carelessly on the floor, where we ourselves or others may tread on it. There is a saying: "If you get too close to a dog, you are likely to get bitten." In the same way, having texts around us all the time can lead to a sense of over-familiarity in which we may neglect to show them due respect. In addition we will find that our mind becomes duller and more ignorant if we fail to pay proper respect to the texts. As the Kadampa masters said: "I have had enough of this ignorance. If I were to become even more ignorant than this, what will happen (to me)?" So we should be careful.

We should be just as careful how we treat magazines which contain something to do with the Buddhist teachings. As a general rule, it is better to avoid stepping over or treading on any written material. However, these days even items like socks and shoes have letters on them, and there are letters also on the road. If we try to avoid stepping on the letters on the road we may get run over by a car, so we do need to discriminate somewhat when following this advice. Be careful not to step over any written information referring to the teachings of Buddha. Discriminating in this way is a good practice to follow.

Going for refuge to the precious Sangha or spiritual community means that we should not form intimate friendships with non-Buddhists and heretics. It is unwise to make a strong connection from our heart with such people for no good purpose, but simply for the sake of food and clothing.

In the past, the great Dom Tonpa and the Bodhisattvas would pick up any stray piece of yellow and red cloth they came across and touch it to their heads, with the thought that whoever wore such cloth must have knowledge. They would meditate on generating faith towards the wearer of the cloth and would carefully store it in a place where no one would step over it. So we should follow their example and always treat monks with respect. Criticising monks earns heavy

66

negativity. It is alright to point out an individual case if one monk has done wrong, but accusing all monks in general of bad behaviour will result in a negative karmic load for us. Laypeople should respect ordained monks as the objects of gaining merit and should develop faith.

From the monk's side, all migratory beings including the gods consider us as an object of refuge and so we have a duty to endeavour to become included among the perfect objects of refuge. Changing our name and our style of dress is nothing special; we need to bring about a change in our mind. We shouldn't be like a person merely wearing the outer garment of a robe, but rather, wearing our robe on the outside we should become a nice monk on the inside. Otherwise, it is hypocrisy to enjoy the possessions and food and drink that people have offered to us. We should act in a good way to benefit both ourself and others, and our actions will become like jewels.

So laypeople should make their offerings with respect and have a pure attitude towards the Sangha, while the Sangha should perform wholesome actions in accordance with their title and purpose. This will become an ornament to the teachings. If the followers of Buddhism enhance the name of Buddha, this benefits the Buddhist teachings in general and will reflect well on us too. This is the seventh practice of a Bodhisattva.

Having taken refuge, we have to follow the general advice on taking refuge, forsaking obstacles and accepting the principle of cause and effect. This means adopting the 10 wholesome deeds by abandoning the 10 unwholesome deeds. The discipline of the 10 wholesome deeds is the discipline of good morals, and it is these deeds that we should practise. This is the eighth practice of a Bodhisattva.

Up to now we have been considering the common graduated path related to the person of small scope. Now we move on to the section of the text which states that the pleasures of cyclic existence are like the dewdrops on the tips of blades of grass, and so forth. This relates to the person of middle scope.

On the graduated path we contemplate the disadvantages of cyclic existence as the truth of suffering, the stages of cyclic existence and the source of suffering, and we learn how to engage in or turn

67

away from cyclic existence. Then we train our mind to attain liberation through the practice of the Three Trainings. We can also develop a good basis for attaining liberation through the eight qualities of fully ripened karma.

Since there is no eternal or long-lasting happiness in cyclic existence:

> Viewing the excellent qualities of cyclic existence as untrustworthy, its unsatisfactory pleasures are the source of all suffering. Therefore, may I be blessed in generating a strong interest to seek the pleasures of liberation.

The worst form of suffering is to enjoy the pleasures of cyclic existence and yet remain dissatisfied. These pleasures, however excellent, are untrustworthy because they are unstable. Fame and position are equally undependable. If there was any certainty in our relationships with beloved relatives and friends, or even with our enemies, that would be proof of something trustworthy in cyclic existence. But there is no such certainty in these relationships, nor is there in our body which also reveals its unreliability.

We have wandered from one life to the next from beginningless time until now, taking various kinds of births. If there had been even one friend who always accompanied us during that wandering, we could trust that person. But there is no such friend. In short, we should contemplate the six drawbacks of cyclic existence, condensed into three,[12] and then do meditation as advised in the 'Graduated Path'. I think the same advice is given in the text known as 'The Basis of All Positive Qualities' and this advice encompasses a great deal.

These words are easy for me to recite and also easy to reflect on. The cause of all our suffering is repeated rebirths. Being conceived again and again involves us in heavy negativity. The cause of these contaminated aggregates of our unfortunate rebirths is karma and afflictions. Until we can cease being conceived over and over again, we continue to take on these contaminated aggregates created by karma and afflictions.

The result of being born in this current, contaminated body is that it provides the conditions for producing new karma and afflictions and functions as the basis of suffering. This body makes us bound to meet

68

with conditions which will increase our afflictions, even when we are not consciously generating them, and it prevents us from applying the antidotes as a method and path leading to enlightenment. These adverse circumstances have accompanied the aggregates since we took birth, and this is the greatest suffering of all.

So we can see that five of the eight sufferings are extremely powerful, namely: the suffering of the birth process; the suffering of being born into adverse circumstances; the suffering of converting birth into affliction; the suffering of being born as the source of suffering; and the suffering of unwilling separation from others which is the nature of the body. This contaminated body is inseparable from us, and it precludes happiness. We should reflect on these things and try our best to become free from cyclic existence.

For this we need to practise according to the Three Trainings without mixing up the order, so that the training in wisdom and concentration rest upon the foundation of the training in morality. We can attain nirvana gradually on this basis by applying antidotes to our afflicted thoughts and their seeds. This relates to the common graduated path for the person of middle capacity. After that, the path of the great vehicle fitting for the person of great capacity is revealed:

> What is the use of our own happiness when all mothers who have been
> Kind to us since beginningless time are suffering?

These sentences, besides being extremely powerful, are the root of the Mahayana teachings, and as such constitute the main point for discussion in this whole text.

As I said yesterday, sentient creatures who are infinite in number and as immeasurable as space share our desire for happiness and the avoidance of suffering. We should be ashamed of ourselves if we only look at our own benefit and disregard their suffering, our hearts unmoved by their torment and our minds unconcerned for them.

Up to now we have been thinking of ourselves as very important, always saying, 'I this...,' 'I that..' and 'I the other...,' and this would be fine if some good resulted from it. But we can see that the self-cherishing attitude is like a chronic disease. An acute medical condition which

69

comes on suddenly may be very severe but can quickly be cured. A chronic disease, on the other hand, is less obvious or severe; but people who are chronically afflicted find themselves unable to eat or drink normally, to move around easily or to work. Such a disease is debilitating and difficult to cure, and has a detrimental effect on their lives.

A self-cherishing attitude is like this chronic disease. We become like only half a person through being afflicted with this attitude, even though we have a mind and the ability to discriminate between right and wrong. So we must put effort into eliminating this chronic disease.

This attitude is described in the 'Mind Training' text as the supreme demon among all other evil spirits. People think that evil spirits and the demons of the external world cause our ruin, and in this human realm where we are born, because of our karma and our prayers, they may appear to be the source of our ill-luck. But this is not actually so. They are not the source of our perpetual ruin; they may harm us on one occasion but will not remain as harmful agents forever, due to the nature of change.

The real cause of our downfall is the self-cherishing attitude because, like that chronic disease, it is always present. An anti-social person in the community, who says unwholesome prayers and is endowed with the 10 drawbacks which should be abandoned, is viewed by practitioners as an object of compassion. Even though he acts like a real enemy and causes trouble, they know that he is only a temporary source of hindrance or affliction to them. Whereas the evil enemy who remains with us constantly is composed of the two false attitudes of self-cherishing and grasping at the self as truly existent. These two support each other like very good friends, as if they have but one heart, and their effect is very damaging. They must be defeated by the wisdom which realises emptiness and the bodhicitta which cherishes others as more important than self. Otherwise these bad attitudes harm us greatly, not only randomly but continually. Each one of them acts like a king with his entourage of attachment, pride, hatred, jealousy, competitiveness, mental dullness, stupor, distraction and laziness. These all work as his courtiers and cause us great harm, so it is not easy for Dharma practitioners to defeat them.

70

Actually, Dharma practitioners are like soldiers in an army. Against whom do we fight? We challenge and defeat the inner enemy of afflictions with which our continuum is endowed, taking up arms against the attitudes of self-cherishing and grasping at true existence. Sometimes we will feel helpless or depressed, because we are challenging the great enemy of all three existences of the mundane realms. It says in the Bodhicharyavatara ('Guide to the Bodhisattva's Way of Life'): "There are many risks involved in fighting a war." This is the nature of war. So when we are fighting a war against the enemy of the afflictions, sometimes we will lose or feel indolent or depressed. But when we continue to challenge this enemy and do not allow ourselves to become utterly depressed we are involved in a truly marvellous activity.

We will experience enormous gain in uprooting the enemy of our afflictions if we challenge our negative attitudes. We can never defeat all our external enemies, as is said in the 'Four Hundred Stanzas': "There never has been a person who died with a relaxed mind, knowing that he has killed everyone he doesn't like. Who is there who only goes on to his next life after eradicating all his enemies?" There is no end to the number of potential external enemies, unless we eradicate our inner enemies. We can put distance between our external enemies and ourselves, yet when they increase their power they will once more be able to harm us. But if we can remove our inner enemies once and for all, they won't reappear.

The Kadampa masters have said that it is the duty of Dharma practitioners to challenge the inimical negative attitudes; in so doing we challenge the enemy of afflictions. One such master, Ban Gungyal, said: "No other way exists to guard the door of the mind than with the trident of the antidotes. When the enemy is strong, I must be on the alert; when it subsides, I relax."

If we hold on to our two negative attitudes of self-cherishing and grasping at inherent existence and we pray in an improper way, some ignorant person may come along who temporarily helps to increase our afflictions; because as long as the negative mind remains, our afflictions can be intensified through contact with an ignorant person (although no one has the ability to cause a permanent increase in our afflictions). Such a person is the opposite of one who assists us in recognising what has to be discarded and what has to accepted, through the clear understanding of all phenomena and the channel of correct reasoning, and who helps us to generate bodhicitta and selflessness.

> The great Munis, who have practised throughout many
> aeons,
> Saw only this (bodhicitta) as beneficial.

It is not necessary to explore in this way for many aeons but, if we do, we will find that the only thing beneficial to sentient beings is bodhicitta, or the attitude of cherishing others as more important than self.

Following this line of thought, we can integrate a kind heart or bodhicitta with the view which realises emptiness, even if we are in a very poor condition, and if we do so we will be wholly victorious in the long-run and will have a solid, trustworthy foundation. For while there is no valid support for the attitudes of self-cherishing and grasping at inherent existence, there is a valid support for the mind which cherishes others as more important than self and the mind which realises emptiness. Moreover, such minds have a strong potential and energy and are supported by the infinite Buddhas of the 10 directions. So whoever has these two kinds of mind in his or her continuum will receive support and protection.

The mind can be made subtly aware through continuous practice, despite the strength of the attitudes of self-cherishing and grasping at the inherent existence of 'I', and this most subtle mind accustomed to positive thought can be transformed into the mind of concentration. The afflictions cannot co-exist with the meditative mind, no matter how powerful they are, and this is something we can justifiably be proud of. So we do not need to become depressed, because we can defeat this self-cherishing attitude by seeing its disadvantages.

> The mind that cherishes all mother beings and seeks to
> secure them in bliss
> Is the gateway to infinite virtues;
> Even if all beings turns out as my enemies,
> May I cherish them more dearly than my own life.

The mind which cherishes others more than self is a source of gaining every imaginable benefit. It can be compared to holy medicine which cures disease, or to a precious substance like nectar. It is our inner spiritual master, the supreme cause of Buddhahood and the unsurpassable remover of the suffering of sentient beings.

Knowing this, we should put every effort into generating this mind of bodhicitta. In cases where such bodhicitta has diminished, it should be restored. Where it has not been diminished, we should work to increase it further. One who is able to expend such effort through the three doors in all phases of day and night has the complete qualities of a true Dharma practitioner and embodies the essence of a human birth in leisure and beneficial circumstances. His or her activities serve as a marvellous offering which will please the enlightened beings as well as purifying negativities and accumulating merit.

> What is the use of our own happiness when all mothers who have been
> Kind to us since beginningless time are suffering?
> Therefore, it is the practice of Bodhisattvas to generate
> Bodhicitta in order to liberate all sentient beings.

This, then, is the 10th practice of a Bodhisattva. The 11th practice of a Bodhisattva consists of contemplating the qualities and drawbacks of the self-cherishing attitude as against the attitude of cherishing others more than self, and training in the practice of exchanging self for others.

Up to now, we have been reviewing what has gone before. Now we will move on:

TWELVE

> If someone, under the power of strong desire, robs or
> Forces others to steal all one's belongings,
> It is the practice of Bodhisattvas to dedicate their body,
> Wealth and the virtues of the three times to them.

This stanza discusses how to train in the practice of exchanging self for others in general, and specifies some of the practices to engage in when ordinary people meet with a condition which gives rise to hatred.

We are likely to feel anger towards someone who robs us or incites others to rob us, out of a strong craving for our possessions. We may be saddened by having lost our possessions, besides which he has no right to deprive us of them; so we may decide to take him to court to try to recover what we have lost. But it says here that a practitioner of the Bodhisattva's way of life should not do such a thing. Rather, it is suggested that we should not only give up our belongings willingly to the one who robs us, but we should also wholeheartedly dedicate to him our body and all our wholesome actions.

Gyalsas Thogmed Zangpo was robbed of all his possessions while en route for Sakya. He requested the fleeing robbers to stop for a moment. Seeing him looking so calm and relaxed, unlike most people who have just been robbed, they stopped in their tracks and he approached them, saying: "Please wait a moment. Just now, when you took my belongings, I didn't get the chance to dedicate them. Now I'd like to do the dedication." Having said this, he dedicated his belongings to the robbers and then he said to them: "If you follow this route, you'll pass by my patron who lives in the valley and he will recognise these things as mine. So you'd better not go this way. Instead, follow that narrow, winding path," and he showed them the safe path. He is known to have actually done this and thus put the words of his text into practice.

THIRTEEN

Even if someone were to cut off one's head,
Without any fault within oneself, it is
The practice of Bodhisattvas to take on all that person's
Negativities with the power of compassion.

The words of this stanza are very difficult to put into practice. Even if we are virtually free of faults, other people, acting out of negative thoughts such as ignorance, jealousy and envy, may approach us with the intention of doing us serious harm, even going so far as

74

to cut off our head. It says here that we should feel compassion rather than anger towards them. We should practise taking on all their negativities accumulated through their hatred and anger, with a spirit of compassion. This reveals the part of the giving and taking practice which relates to taking.

FOURTEEN

Even if someone were to shout different types of insults
At oneself throughout the three thousand worlds,
It is the practice of Bodhisattvas still to speak
Of that person's good qualities with a loving mind.

This refers to a situation in which, out of feelings of antagonism towards us, someone not only spreads harsh rumours about us behind our back to a few people, but also propagates these unpleasant words throughout the three thousand worlds. We would normally feel angry that he is belittling us, pointing out our faults and despising us. But the Mahayana practitioner should not think in this way. Rather, even though he has announced our mistakes to the world at large, we should regard him with a loving mind, speak of the knowledge he possesses and praise him.

FIFTEEN

Even if someone were to uncover one's most intimate
faults and say harsh words in the
Centre of a crowd of many people, it is the practice of
Bodhisattvas to bow humbly to that person,
With the thought that he is a spiritual master.

There may be one person in the crowd here who harbours ill-intent towards us and belittles us in public, exposing our weak points and saying negative things about us. This makes us blush and feel the discomfort of guilt, and we may also become angry. But actually this person is very important to us. We are not aware of all our weaknesses, so this person is like our spiritual master in pointing them out to us. Even though he is acting out of ill-will, we should think of him as being very kind and should not feel anger towards him.

It is said that we should see the lama's instructions as highlighting our negative aspects. We should view all the negativities accumulated via the three doors in the mirror of Dharma and should set about eliminating these negativities of the three doors in the correct manner. Just as we try to heed our lama's instructions regarding our weak points, so should we consider the ordinary person who talks about our weaknesses as equal to a spiritual master and should dwell on his kindness.

It is bad to be praised and good to be despised.

Our own weakness is directly pointed out when we are despised. So, as it says here, rather than enjoying being praised, we should be glad to be despised. Why is this so? Because the disadvantage of receiving praise is that our pride is increased. But if someone despises us, we try our best to overcome the faults of which we are accused. By being confronted with our faults, we feel ashamed of them and adopt an attitude of trying to avoid them in the future.

Similarly, it is said that:

It's bad to be happy and good to suffer; when we suffer
We remember the holy Dharma. When we are happy,
We exhaust our previously accumulated merit.

These sayings are actually connected with the core of the practice.

SIXTEEN

Even if a person whom one has cared for lovingly
Like one's own son were to regard one as an enemy,
It is the practice of Bodhisattvas to show greater kindness,
Like a mother to her son who is stricken by an illness.

The meaning of this stanza is also to be found in the 'Eight Verses on the Training of the Mind' by Geshe Langri Thangpa: "When one whom I have helped and of whom I have great expectations treats me with unkindness, may I hold him as my supreme guru." We may nurture and support someone like our own son, with such loving concern that we deserve to be repaid, yet find that he chooses to abuse us or treat us as his enemy instead of repaying our kindness. Similarly, in the 'Four Hundred Stanzas' it says:

76

Someone who behaves badly because of being possessed
    by a demon
Will not evoke anger in the doctors looking after him.
Just so, Muni sees affliction as the enemy rather than
The person who acts out of the affliction.

And in 'The Amazing Praise' by Changkya Rolpai Dorje it says:

The son who is afflicted by devils may scold his loving
    mother,
But she continues to show him love and concern.
Similarly, when these migratory beings of the degenerate
    era abuse you,
You the compassionate one regard them with loving
    kindness.

When the Minister Giwang showed grave disrespect and effrontery towards the Seventh Dalai Lama Kelsang Gyatso, for example, His Holiness Kelsang Gyatso displayed not the slightest trace of anger towards his minister but demonstrated a wholly compassionate and loving mind. This is why Changkya Rolpai Dorje wrote these prayers, in praise of His Holiness the Seventh Dalai Lama.

The mother whose son is possessed by a demon and threatens her with a knife does not become angry. Instead she does her utmost to remove the demon's influence from her son. Similarly, if someone I have helped and nurtured with kindness turns around and insults me, instead of generating anger towards him I should sincerely try to eliminate his afflictions. These things are extremely difficult to put into practice, which is why they are discussed in separate stanzas of the text, in order to emphasise them.

SEVENTEEN

Even if a person of the same or lower status than oneself
Were to attempt to insult one out of arrogance,
It is the practice of Bodhisattvas respectfully to take
That person, like a guru, on the top of their heads.

This means that we should treat the person who harms or insults us out of pride as our lama and bow to him with respect. Even if his knowledge and lifestyle are the same or lesser than ours, or if under normal circumstances he couldn't hope to compete with us in any way, this is a very beneficial practice.

When such a person arouses our anger and that anger remains with us for one or two days, it's a good idea to visualise that person in front of us and recite the following words over and over again, from the 'Eight Verses of Mind Training' by Geshe Langri Thangpa:

> Whenever I associate with others,
> May I, from the depths of my heart,
> Think of myself as the lowest of all
> And of all others as supreme.

While reciting these words and visualising the person in front of us, we should touch our head to his feet with the thought, "I am lower than you. Compared to me you are supreme in such-and-such knowledge and for this reason and that reason you are higher than me."

Thinking in this way will benefit our mind by making it calmer. After some time we will find that the fierce anger in our mind towards him reduces in intensity and becomes powerless. If we feel some loss of dignity in this process, we can keep this to ourselves and, when we meet him, simply act naturally. We should treat him like our lama in our visualisation practice, respecting him and prostrating to him, with the purpose of achieving calmness in our mind.

It is said that the greatest hindrances in the practice of Dharma arise either when we are extremely weak or extremely powerful. This point is emphasised in the Bodhicharyavatara ('Guide to the Bodhisattva's Way of Life'). There is a risk of our Dharma practice degenerating when we become very weak or, alternatively, very successful, so that we are not able to hold on to it properly. We must be vigilant at these times.

For example, at present we Tibetans have had to leave our homeland. We are scattered around the world and face a shortage of food and drink. People humiliate us by calling us refugees. On top of that, we may be someone who has caught tuberculosis and is hospitalised. We may also experience some afflictions from our regional deity and we become depressed, thinking, "I have lost my

78

country and my monastery. I am sick and people ridicule me. If I recite prayers now, it won't help. Whatever I do now won't help me. I am weak and I lack the basic necessities of life. If I just had some friends to take care of me, I wouldn't mind all these other things; but I have no friends.

"On top of that, I am bullied by others. If I was healthy, I wouldn't mind but I am not healthy, I am tormented by terrrible disease. Even though this is so, if my mind was more stable and not possessed by demons, it would be okay. But demons have possessed my mind and so I am altogether in a hopeless state with all these things afflicting me."

It is easy to forget the practice of a Bodhisattva when we are in a situation like this, so we should be very careful at such times. How can we do this?

EIGHTEEN

Even if one has a poor livelihood, is always insulted by people
And is afflicted by a very severe illness or evil spirits,
It is still the practice of Bodhisattvas undauntedly to take on
The negativities and sufferings of all living beings.

Whatever suffering we ourselves endure, we should wish for the sufferings of all sentient beings to ripen on to it, thinking, "May this suffering of mine represent and purify all the sufferings of sentient beings." We should generate great inner strength without losing courage, so that we may take on the actual sufferings of others and the negativities which are their root cause. This practice of the Bodhisattvas is extremely important.

There is also a chance of neglecting the Dharma if we become successful and gain a lot of possessions. Therefore, it is said:

NINETEEN

Even if one is famous, respected by many and with the
wealth of Vishravana (the guardian king),
It is the practice of Bodhisattvas, having seen
The essencelessness of the glory and wealth
Of worldly existence, to remain without pride.

We may develop a reputation for knowing the texts as well as for
our general knowledge, so that people praise us. We may become very
popular and even be featured on the front page of the newspapers. This
popularity we have gained has not come about because of our
notoriety, such as murdering or harming others, but from earning a
good reputation. And so people bow their heads in respect to us and
out of affection for us.

In addition, we want for nothing. We have so many worldly
possessions that we can compete even with the richest person of all.
We have loyal assistants and good friends, and many people follow
us in order to serve us. At this time, the practice of the Bodhisattvas
may degenerate, and we may start to think along these lines: "I have
many possessions and a good reputation. I am very educated, and
people praise me out of their respect and trust in me."

We may know something of what the Buddhist scriptures say,
but there is a danger that we will develop an unhealthy attitude
which leads us to think, "I know this much of the texts and I have a
scholarly reputation as such-and-such. I know the texts so well that
if Nagarjuna himself came here now, I would be able to defeat him.
Even if Manjushri were to come, it would be okay." We begin to
think that even if we were face to face with the six ornaments and the
two supreme teachers,[13] we would conduct ourselves well, and we
don't realise that this kind of thinking heralds our entry into the hell
realms. Various kinds of non-Dharma thoughts may also arise through
people placing their faith and respect in us.

Similarly, if we are very brave and mentally strong, we may start
to think in this way: "I have worked so hard for the sake of Dharma
and politics, so if I accumulate some negativities it doesn't matter."
There's a danger in such thoughts, because it is probable that we
won't be able to practise the Dharma properly while inflated with

80

pride and pompous in manner, relying on the incorrect reasoning. We should be very careful indeed at such times.

As is written in the 'Engagement of Faith', the biography of Je Rinpoche: "When people lay down a special carpet for me and make many offerings out of reverence, their respect is genuine; despite that, in that very instant I spontaneously recognise that all these things are impermanent and untrustworthy, as deceptive as an illusion. With this thought I feel immensely sad, seeing all appearances as insubstantial and transitory. This enduring sadness brings about a transformation in the depths of my heart, which has been innate from the very beginning.

"One should follow the advice given in the Bodhicharyavatara ('Guide to the Bodhisattva's Way of Life') which says: 'Why like someone who praises you, when there is bound to be someone else who despises you? Similarly, there's no point in disliking someone who despises you, because there are others who praise you.' These truly are compassionate words and we should heed them. Without investigating the matter, I feel that praise has the nature of suffering. The transformation brought about in the depths of my mind stays with me for a long time and in fact has been innate since long ago."

This passage contains profound wisdom. For what is the point of clinging to the empty fame of a great reputation? What is so wonderful about praise? It is merely dry words. Someone may praise us today, but if we then do something unworthy that praise becomes useless. This is discussed in the 'Precious Garland' and likewise in the 'Instructions to a King' by Nagarjuna, where it is said that one's reputation, however great, is nothing wonderful in itself.

Nor should we crave or be attached to our belongings, even if we have many. Accumulating and protecting possessions and fame is said to be the cause of much suffering. We should call to mind the good things of cyclic existence one by one and consider their disadvantages, and in this way tame our minds to avoid becoming inflated with pride. As 'Brom sTonpa said: "You should remain humble while being praised extravagantly and take an easy approach to what pleases you."

This is an extremely significant saying, and I practise this as much as possible. People present offerings, pay their respects and praise me, saying, "This is His Holiness the Dalai Lama," but I

81

maintain my humility. It is my duty as a single monk to engage my mind wholly in the Dharma and doing so also makes me happy.

Others should do likewise. For example, you shouldn't fight for a good position in the seating arrangement nor hope for it, but should rather give up this way of thinking. You should engage in Dharma activities which are real Dharma practice. "One may be engaged in non-Dharma while wearing the outward trappings of Dharma." You should be mindful constantly and perform self-assessment as often as possible. Check yourself as far as you can; if you really cannot do this then it is not your fault.

Being humble and taking a low position results in blissful happiness, and is extremely important. If we try to maintain a high position, we will experience unhappiness later if things do not work out as we had hoped; whereas we will not have to experience any sense of loss from choosing to adopt a lowly position. Humility is particularly important in the Tibetan community, where we have good examples to follow.

However, people in societies where it is not regarded as admirable to seek a lowly position do suffer losses by adopting a humble stance. Such social customs cannot be trusted, when people who hold a low position are seen as unfit to shoulder the responsibilities of society. These people earn only insults and humiliation from sticking to their humble attitude. This is different from Tibetan society, where these problems do not as yet occur. So for Tibetans it is better to be humble, and this is especially significant for those who have titles and the name of a scholar, Geshe, lama and so forth. A humble attitude is a beautiful decoration for the teachings, whereas the pride and arrogance that can come from having a title doesn't reflect well on the Dharma.

Whatever people choose to do, that's up to them. It's no business of mine. But because we have freedom of speech, I have chosen to say these things. Arrogant people do not make a good impression and such pride is essenceless. I have several friends who belittle and insult others based on what little they know, although they do not recognise their own faulty judgments. So it is the practice of a Bodhisattva to forsake pride, as is said here. Now we can move on to the next verse.

TWENTY

If outer enemies are destroyed while not restraining
The enemy of one's own hatred, the outer enemies will
   increase.
Therefore, it is the practice of Bodhisattvas to conquer
Their own minds with the powerful army of love and
   compassion.

All the external enemies we vanquish will endlessly be replaced by others if we do not tame the hatred within us. It is said in the Bodhicharyavatara ('Guide to the Bodhisattva's Way of Life'):

Where would I possibly find enough leather
With which to cover the surface of the earth?
But (wearing) leather just on the soles of my shoes
Is equivalent to covering the earth with it.

The meaning is:

Unruly beings are as (unlimited) as space:
They cannot possibly all be overcome.
But if I overcome thoughts of anger alone,
This will be equivalent to vanquishing all foes.

How can we subdue all our enemies in this mundane realm of three thousand worlds? It is impossible. However, taming the inner enemy of anger is equivalent to taming all external enemies. For example, in modern China there has been a lot of trouble from 1959 onwards, because of ministers competing with each other for control; so something is not right. If we consider this situation from the point of view of Dharma, we can see that while our inner anger remains untamed we lack endurance or forbearance. Things may go smoothly for a few days or months; then a problem occurs which has to be dealt with, and then another problem crops up to take its place. This is readily apparent. So in China, from 1959 to 1969 and again from 1973 to '74, there was no peace.

There is a lot of trouble in politics generally, the source of which is untamed inner anger. As a result people are unable to overcome the external enemies around them, let alone the enemies of a different

83

country. Difficulties arise because people vie for control over each other. The answer to this is to have control over our inner enemy of anger. But how can we achieve this?

Without wielding an arrow, weapon and shield,
One subjugates a billion Maras entirely by oneself.
Who knows this war technique other than you?

We have to tame our inner enemy by adopting the armour of love and the immense power of compassion. So, in the Tibetan community, we should be frank and polite to each other, speaking face to face and making a clear distinction between right and wrong. By acting in such a way we can gradually overcome the angry outbursts of others and calm them down. It only makes matters worse if we retaliate with anger when others show their anger to us, just as stirring up muddy water makes it more murky and of no use to anyone. But behaving politely defuses anger after some time. Bouts of rage serve no purpose other than to increase people's anger, pride, jealousy and competitiveness.

Making strong divisions between ourselves and our own side as against others and their side increases the likelihood of spontaneous outbursts of anger. In the face of anger, we should give a reasoned explanation if the other person is receptive. But if he or she doesn't want to listen, then leave it for the time being.

Anger is an unstable emotion. It arises without warning and fades after a while. Even though he is the person he always was, a person filled with anger will not be swayed by his relatives attempting to console him. He will still hit his enemy on the head. Later, when his anger has faded, they may even become friends.

We can see from this example that the inner enemy is extremely harmful. Separate explanations are given in this discussion of taming the enemy of our afflictions on how to apply the antidotes to anger and to hatred. It is emphasised that there is great harm in leaving the mind tainted by hatred. In the next verse, we are shown how to apply the antidote to attachment.

TWENTY ONE

Sensual pleasures, like salt water, increase desire
No matter how much they are enjoyed.
So the practice of Bodhisattvas is immediately to abandon
All objects that generate a desire towards them.

This refers to the objects of desire such as form, sound, smell, taste and touch. However much we enjoy the pleasures of these objects of desire, it is as if we were drinking salty water, which only increases our longing for more water. Likewise, indulging in the pleasures of desire only serves to increase passion. For instance, it seems that sexual intercourse gives pleasure temporarily but leads to dissatisfaction in the long run. It's like an itchy skin disease which we scratch to bring relief and pleasure. This works for a while, but then we have to go on scratching until the skin has open wounds and is bleeding. As it says in the 'Precious Garland':

Scratching itchy skin which is diseased brings pleasure,
But it's more pleasurable not to have the skin disease.
Similarly, mundane people gain pleasure from desire,
But it's more pleasurable to be free from desire.

There's no lasting satisfaction at all in the gratification of desires. However much we enjoy them at the time, they will increase our clinging. It is the practice of a Bodhisattva to reflect on the disadvantages of the qualities of desire and the objects which evoke desire in us and then repeatedly abandon these objects.

Prior to this the text has been dealing with the practices related to conventional bodhicitta. Here it seems it is discussing the entrance to the practice of ultimate bodhicitta, which has two aspects: practising space-like equipoise in meditation, and practising post-meditational awareness of the illusory nature of phenomena.

TWENTY TWO

Whatever appears is (the manifestation of) one's own
    mind;
The nature of mind itself is primordially free from fabri-
    cation.
Knowing this, it is the practice of Bodhisattvas
Not to conceive the signs of object and subject.

Whatever appears to us is mere mind—both the phenomena of
the cyclic realms and those realms beyond the cyclic. This is either a
way of saying that external phenomena are a part of the mind, which
is related to the Chittamatrin school (or Mind Only school) or the
view of Yogacharya Svatantrika Madhyamika.

If I explain it according to the view of the esteemed Chandrakirti,
it means that phenomena of both the mundane and non-mundane
realms which appear in their various pure and impure aspects are all
devoid of inherent existence. This view holds that they are established
subjectively by the conventional mind and exist merely by virtue of
being labelled. If a phenomenon truly and concretely exists from its
own side as it appears to us, then its true existence should become
clearer and clearer when we examine it by its label. Yet in actuality,
when we examine it closely, instead of its existence becoming more
obvious we discover that its nature is not to be found.

Do we fail to find its nature because the phenomenon does exist
or because it doesn't exist? It is not because of its non-existence that we
are unable to find it. It has a function and therefore it must exist. The
wholesome or unwholesome effect that it has upon our environment
and upon beings also testifies to its existence. We can see it for
ourselves because it exists in our line of vision. So we can deduce that
it is not because of its non-existence that we fail to locate its nature.
We can be quite sure that it does exist.

But if we go on exploring, looking for its objective existence, we
do not find it. We would be able to find it if it had independent
existence; therefore we can deduce that it cannot exist objectively, but
rather comes into existence naturally through the conventional mind.

When the purity or impurity of phenomena appear to our
present mind, do they appear from their own side or how do they

86

appear to us? To our way of thinking, the object's appearance seems to originate from its own side, and in this way our minds adopt a mistaken view. As the Seventh Dalai Lama said:

> To a consciousness overpowered by sleep
> A dream-object appears. Yet there's no real object there,
> Merely an appearance designated by the mind.

Giving the example of dream and magical appearance, whatever appears at that time has no true inherent existence. For example, we may dream of a herd of elephants, but there's no actual herd of elephants there. Or we may dream of Tibet, but in that dream the land of Tibet does not actually exist; it is mere appearance. As it is said:

> There is nothing truly existent within the basis of
> Imputation. There are only the labels bestowed
> By the deluded consciousness upon entities such as
> Self and others, cyclic existence, nirvana and so forth.

Although it seems that cyclic existence, nirvana and so forth exist within the basis of imputation, they have no objective existence that we can point our finger at and say, "This is this," or, "This is that."

Still then it is said that:

> The torpid lassitude of ignorance in the
> Ordinary person's consciousness attributes
> A solid and true existence to objects.
> Look at the activity of this disgusting mind of ours.

A mind afflicted by ignorance, which is like torpor invading the ordinary person's consciousness, apprehends phenomena as existing objectively from their own side. We are invited to examine this in the light of our own experience, to discover that our disgusting minds, familiarised with ignorance from beginningless time, apprehend all objects as having independent existence. We do not see them as existing through the power of naming and worldly designation.

The objects to which we point, saying, "This is this," or, "This is that," appear to exist from their own side in a solid, concrete and independent fashion. They appear so without having such existence.

As it is said:

> The true existence of the 'I', which has appeared
> To the deluded mind from the very beginning of time,
> Is the subtle object which needs to be negated. It is vital
> Completely to refute this mistaken notion in one's mind.

The various pure and impure aspects of appearance are all mind only, or exist due to the mind, and also exist due to labelling and the mind, but do not exist from the side of the objects themselves.

Likewise, mind itself is included among all other phenomena. If we investigate the mind, dividing it into previous and later moments and searching for it according to its label, we cannot find it. Taking the eye consciousness as an example, which appears concrete to our minds, we can divide it into its parts and find that it has no entity separate from these parts. Each part cannot be said to be the same as the entire entity, because the whole entity and the parts are different from each other. In a similar way, if we divide the limbs of the body into their separate parts, we won't find the possessor of those limbs. Although it exists, it does so only in reliance upon the limbs themselves.

Exploring meticulously in this way, we come to the stage where there is nothing we can confidently point to, and we conclude that mind itself is pure from the very beginning and free from extremes.

> It neither exists nor does it not exist.
> It is neither nor both,
> Nor is it separate from them.

Things which are in the nature of mere non-inherent existence and free from extremes are as described here:

> All phenomena of both the mundane and the non-
> mundane realms
> Are merely imputed by our inner mind.
> Exploring that mind as well, it is free from arising and
> Ceasing. Thus, the nature of reality is wonderful.

All mundane and non-mundane phenomena are merely labelled by the mind and mind itself, when it is explored, is free from arising and ceasing. Likewise, the nature of the person endowed with a

88

mind is non-inherent arising. "I, the truly non-existent practitioner of space-like emptiness, see that in reality nothing exists intrinsically. All visual and auditory appearances are revealed as illusory pictures, and from this union of delightful appearance and emptiness I have become convinced incontrovertibly of dependent arising." That great, truly non-existent yogi, when apprehending all visual, auditory and cognising appearances, sees that they don't exist.

If all these appearances possessed inherent existence, there could be no contradiction in them. Let us take the example of a tree: in summer there is an increase in its foliage, and so forth. Then comes monsoon followed by winter when the weather is dry and cold. In summer the tree is very beautiful, yet in winter it is quite ugly. If the tree's qualities truly existed within itself, how could this change occur? How could an attractive tree be transformed into an ugly one?

Similarly, how could a person who at present is handsome and youthful become old and infirm? Also, if our deluded mind truly existed, how could it be transformed into the mind of enlightenment which is possessed of complete knowledge and has abandoned every negativity? The one who is tainted with faults and the faults themselves, the qualities of attractiveness and its opposite, of beauty and ugliness—all these various aspects can exist without contradiction because of non-inherent existence.

If there was true existence, how could causes and conditions influence it? And how would it be possible for results to accrue? How could effects be reliant upon causes? It is clear that there are causes and conditions, and good and bad. These can only occur because of non-inherent existence and thus it is decisively proven that phenomena lack true or inherent existence. Hence the quotation given earlier: "I, the truly non-existent practitioner of space-like emptiness, see that in reality nothing exists intrinsically. All visual and auditory appearances are revealed as illusory pictures, and from this union of delightful appearance and emptiness I have become convinced incontrovertibly of dependent arising."

The arising of unmistakable appearances indicates that form is emptiness. It is because phenomena lack inherent existence that a transformation occurs dependent upon their conditions, so that various aspects of phenomena can appear to us. Therefore it is clear that appearance does not negate emptiness, nor does emptiness negate appearance.

> Just by seeing irrefutable dependent arising,
> Spontaneously and without any effort all
> The previous ways of apprehending objects completely
>   dissolve and
> Exploration of the view is completely accomplished.

Although I do not understand this precisely, nevertheless I think that this is the case.

We need to have a well-established familiarity with this view in our minds in order to apprehend appearance and emptiness without contradiction and in a complementary relationship to each other. We need to develop conviction in both the emptiness aspect, which is non-inherent existence, and in the appearance aspect of phenomena. We must examine the emptiness aspect again and again to deepen our conviction. When we understand some of the techniques in realising dependent arising we should analyse how our minds apprehend objects and direct our efforts principally towards recognising the object of negation. Then when the object of negation becomes clearer, we analyse the non-inherent existence of phenomena, using the reasoning of normal conceptual thought applied to these phenomena.

We should employ these complementary techniques to think about and explore the emptiness and appearance aspects, not just for one or two days but continuously. If we do so, there is a chance that we will come to see these two, appearance and emptiness, as complementary to each other. Understanding conceptual imputation in such a way is highly beneficial.

If an object existed by itself without relying upon the mind, it would have to appear and exist in a unique way. But we find that it does not exist in any unique fashion when we investigate it. The fact that it does not actually exist like this arises convincingly in the depths of our mind and at this time the concrete existence of the object may dissolve, as if we have truly understood the nature of reality.

In addition, we should be able to rest our minds on that understanding with tranquillity. Without good stability of mind we will find it difficult to rest our minds for long without losing touch with

90

that understanding we have gained. Resting our minds momentarily may allow for a glimpse of voidness to arise, but it is not possible for the various aspects of phenomena to appear in that moment. So, by knowing voidness:

> We do not hold the signs of both the
> Knower and the known in our minds.

The meaning of emptiness is explained here. It is said that not seeing (in a deluded way) is the supreme seeing. Resting our minds with ease on such reality is a way of practising space-like meditative equipoise.

Now we can consider the post-meditational practice of the awareness of the magical appearance of phenomena. The author discusses this subject in relation to the two objects of attachment and anger.

TWENTY THREE

> It is the practice of Bodhisattvas to renounce
> Clinging attachment when meeting with pleasant objects;
> For although they appear beautiful, like a rainbow in
> summer,
> They should not be seen as truly existent.

The purpose and effect of realising emptiness is to relate to objects in a balanced fashion, so we must become aware of the reality of phenomena in order to achieve that. Once we understand the mode of existence of phenomena—their deceptive appearance and actual lack of inherent existence—detachment from the belief in their intrinsic existence arises. We will never be deceived when we know the deceptive nature of their appearance and relate to it properly.

Once we have become convinced of emptiness we are reluctant to allow the various pure and impure aspects of phenomena to arise in our mind. Their appearance leads to grasping at their intrinsic existence, and this is exaggerated by misconceptions which evoke attachment and anger. The reality of various aspects of phenomena is established here in order to refute such misconceptions.

Having ascertained the nature of reality during meditative equipoise, we find that we do not abandon discriminating awareness of good and bad during the post-meditation period, when contemplating the various aspects of objects. If we lean too much towards only the good so that we see unqualified goodness, attachment arises conditioned by misconceptions—such attachment is to be given up.

Ignorance and grasping at inherent existence need to work together if attachment is to arise. The exact opposite of the mind which grasps at inherent existence is the mind which has a firm conviction of non-inherent existence. If the energy, influence and constancy of such a conviction are present, then even when we come across something attractive during the post-meditational period we see that object, which is as beautiful as a rainbow in summer, as not being truly existent. This occurs by virtue of the power of our strong conviction in non-inherent existence gained during meditative equipoise. We fail to create an intense craving towards that object by seeing its true, non-intrinsic nature; gradually, in this way, we overcome the tendency to grasp at the true existence of phenomena. If the grasping does not arise, attachment also fails to be evoked.

Hatred and attachment are invariably accompanied by ignorance. As it says in the root text of the 'Four Hundred Stanzas':

> Just as the body's sense faculties pervade the whole body,
> So does ignorance exist in all the afflictions.
> Thus, every single delusion will be stamped out
> By dispelling ignorance.

This can be explained by reference to the eminent Chandrakirti's unique assertion of the ways to recognise negativities. Generally speaking, there are two ways to go about abandoning attachment—seeing the ugliness of a once beautiful object, and seeing attractive objects as lacking true existence. There is a difference in power between these two. Meditating on ugliness as an antidote to attachment has less power in uprooting attachment than does generating a strong conviction in non-inherent existence. Employing both methods is extremely effective, and understanding reality in this way is a marvellous step on the road to attaining nirvana.

TWENTY FOUR

The various sufferings are like the death of a son in a
dream.
There is weariness due to holding illusive appearances as
real.
Therefore, when meeting with unfavourable conditions it
is the practice of
Bodhisattvas to view them as illusory.

This explains how to view both the hatred-inducing object and suffering as a dream. Various aspects of suffering can be seen as deceptive and illusory, like the death of a son in a dream. It is said that we will greatly benefit by being able to overcome our grasping at true existence.

Here we have been discussing the ways of practising absolute bodhicitta. From now on, the author explains the practice of the six perfections.

TWENTY FIVE

If it is necessary to give up even one's body when seeking
enlightenment,
What need is there to mention giving up external
objects?
Therefore, it is the practice of Bodhisattvas to be
Generous without hoping for reward or ripening merit.

What mention needs to be made of sacrificing material goods, when those who intend to attain supreme Buddhahood for the sake of sentient beings have to be prepared to sacrifice their very lives? However, if we practise generosity with the secret intention of gaining wealth and fame, this is related to the mind which seeks self-benefit and is not the generosity practised by the Bodhisattvas since their generosity is not tainted by self-concern. We should be generous with the sole intention of benefitting others, and the results accrued by such generous acts should be dedicated from the depths of our heart to the welfare of others. One practising this kind of generosity does not expect to be repaid nor to gain good ripening results; such is the generosity practised by a Bodhisattva.

TWENTY SIX

If through lacking moral discipline, one cannot achieve
one's own purpose,
It is laughable to want to benefit others. Therefore
It is the practice of Bodhisattvas, who have no craving
For worldly pleasure, to preserve moral discipline.

It seems that this is based on one passage in the Sutra Alankara and contains the essence of it. We need to aim gradually for a higher rebirth in order to benefit other beings, for without that we will be handicapped in this work. Since the sole cause for attaining the body of a higher rebirth such as a human being is good moral conduct, we must practise ethical discipline. It is laughable to think of working for other beings unless we have the body of a higher rebirth—how can we benefit others if we cannot control ourselves properly?

The self-benefitting mind acts out of desire for the pleasures of cyclic existence, preserving morality in order to avoid rebirth in the lower realms and to attain a higher rebirth. A Bodhisattva, on the other hand, preserves morality not with these intentions but rather to attain a higher rebirth in order to benefit others. Therefore, it is the practice of Bodhisattvas to challenge their inner afflictions with greater determination even than the hearers and solitary realisers do.

TWENTY SEVEN

To Bodhisattvas, who desire the wealth of virtue, all
agents of harm
Are like a precious treasure. Therefore, cultivating
The patience that is free from hatred and animosity
Towards all is the practice of Bodhisattvas.

Patience is the main practice of a Bodhisattva. To the Bodhisattva who longs for the accumulation of wholesome deeds, all the three kinds of people—lowly, middle and high-ranking—who inflict harm

94

are like the source of precious treasure. Interacting with them causes the practice of patience to develop. So because of this the Bodhisattva practises patience free from resentment towards all, both high and low.

In the Sutra Alankara we find the statement: "Patience amongst all..."

These words are extremely powerful. When we are belittled by someone in a position of authority, we may tell others that we are practising patience in the face of such humiliation. But actually we have no alternative but to practise patience in this instance, since we are in the inferior position. The real practice of patience, however, is towards those lower than ourselves, because we are able to retaliate but we choose not to do so.

TWENTY EIGHT

If even Shravakas and Pratyekabuddhas, working for self
gain,
Are seen to make efforts as if their heads were on fire,
It is the practice of Bodhisattvas to benefit all beings by
Expending joyous effort, the source of all good qualities.

Even hearers and solitary realisers, who practise out of self-concern, exert tremendous effort as if their heads had caught fire. So Bodhisattvas, who intend to lead all migratory beings to the supreme state of Buddhahood, must practise joyous effort—which is the source of all knowledge—more fervently even than these hearers and solitary realisers.

TWENTY NINE

Through having realised that calm abiding in combina-
tion with
Special insight completely destroys afflictions,
It is the practice of Bodhisattvas to train in the
Concentration which surpasses the four formless stages.

We are taught to practise concentration for the purpose of uprooting cyclic existence, by relying upon the wisdom which understands emptiness supported by the calm abiding mind. This concentration differs from the path characterised by calm abiding

95

and special insight which is part of the four states of absorption of the form realms. In this context it refers to the type of concentration found in the union of special insight and calm abiding of the mind which realises emptiness, which uproots cyclic existence and goes beyond the path of the four states of absorption. So it is said that we must train single-pointedly in such concentration in order to achieve it.

THIRTY

It is the practice of Bodhisattvas to train in the
Wisdom supported by method that does not
Conceptualise the three spheres; without wisdom one
    will be unable
To achieve complete Buddhahood by means of the five
    perfections.

Lacking wisdom is like lacking eyes to focus with. We won't derive much benefit even from the sincere practice of everything from generosity to contemplation if our mind is obscured and without wisdom, nor will we create the cause for enlightenment. Therefore, we should practise the development of wisdom. I'm not referring to wisdom alone here, but wisdom supported by method and method upheld by wisdom. These two should not be separated. Based on these we have to practise the two accumulations of merit and wisdom. Supported by method, we should realise the non-inherent existence of the doer, the deed itself and the recipient of the deed. Practising the wisdom which understands this non-inherent existence is said to be the practice of a Bodhisattva.

THIRTY ONE

With (merely) the external appearance of a practitioner, if
    one does not
Examine one's own mistakes, one may act in opposition
    to the Dharma.
Therefore, it is the practice of Bodhisattvas always
To examine one's own mistakes and abandon them.

96

This training in mindfulness is explained here as well as in the chapters on wisdom and conscientiousness in the Bodhi- charyavatara ('Guide to the Bodhisattva's Way of Life'). We must examine our mistakes, for we run the risk of committing non-Dharma acts out of carelessness, while ostensibly being Dharma practitioners. For instance, we monks bear the title of Dharma practitioner and present such an image to the world. But despite this, we may become involved in acts of a non-Dharma nature. So we should try our best to abandon our mistakes through seeing them clearly.

THIRTY TWO

If, due to the power of afflictions, one were to discuss
The faults of other Bodhisattvas, one would degenerate.
Therefore, not speaking of the faults of others who
Abide in the Mahayana is the practice of Bodhisattvas.

Extensive negativities accrue from discussing the faults of others. As it says in the Sutra of Self-Liberation or Prati Moksha:

We must examine right and wrong within ourselves,
And the level of our own awareness,
Rather than examining the faults,
Deeds and misdeeds of others.

We must investigate our own state of awareness. Sometimes it happens that out of compassion we talk about the virtues and non-virtues of others and whether they are aware or not; but pointing out others' drawbacks and hiding our own faults is not Dharma. This is particularly important for those who practise Mahayana Dharma with faith and live in a place where these teachings flourish; if we point out others' failings we may unknowingly be speaking about Bodhisattvas, since it can be difficult to recognise them. Discussing the faults of Bodhisattvas leads to the downfall of those involved in such negative talk. Those who engage in Mahayana practice and do not discuss others' faults are following the practice of the Bodhisattvas.

Je Gedun Drup also speaks of the need for a pure outlook:

> In general, contemplate the kindness of all sentient beings,
> And in particular train your mind in pure thoughts
> About all who practise the Dharma.
> There is an enemy inside you; subdue your delusion.

It is the responsibility of Mahayana practitioners generally to recognise the kindness of all sentient beings and to contemplate that kindness, just as it is improper to harbour thoughts of clinging or hatred.

We must refrain from accumulating negativities in relation to the Dharma, and eschew actions which cause us to abandon it. We should not discriminate by saying, "He is Nyingma," "He is Kagyud," "He is an ascetic," or "He is such-and-such." In the past it was said that, "Scholars are held in high regard by other scholars."

When scholars make critiques and various assertions, using logic and texts, for the sake of upholding, protecting, promoting and refining their own Dharma, these are not made out of hatred or attachment. Rather, they are stated in order to clear up confusions and for the purpose of thorough investigation, just as gold is tested by cutting, rubbing and burning it. But if the scholars' followers, possessing only limited knowledge, involve themselves in criticism of others out of hatred or attachment; if they compose texts in which they criticise each other; and if they indulge in backbiting about one another, they are creating divisions in their community and leading others astray. These unwholesome deeds, which come about through the Dharma, are pernicious.

So we should take the opposite approach to this and train our mind in a pure outlook towards every Dharma practitioner. We may feel we have certain skills and talents, but we should not flaunt these in front of others; we should use them instead to subdue the inner enemies of our delusions. This is really good advice expressed here in a helpful and pleasing manner.

Once, when Je Gedun Drup was old, he uttered some melancholy words. His companions said to him: "You don't need to feel so upset. After finishing this life, you will certainly be reborn in Tushita. This was prophesied a long time ago." Je Gedun Drup replied: "I neither

98

intend nor aspire to be reborn in Tushita. My only wish is to be reborn in this impure realm so that I can benefit flawed sentient creatures as much as I can." These are the words of a Bodhisattva, and it really helps us to hear them. (I should mention that his speech is greatly condensed here.)

THIRTY THREE

Material offerings and gifts cause arguments among
    people, and degenerate the
Actions of listening, contemplating and meditating.
So it is the practice of Bodhisattvas to abandon
Attachment to the households of friends and patrons.

This has occurred in the history of Tibet, when those people who sincerely worked for the Dharma were obstructed by political conflict. Take the example of the omnisicient Lama Jamyang Shadpa, an immeasurably high lama of Amdo province, considered by the people of Amdo to be an emanation of Je Rinpoche, and as supreme as Vajrasattva himself. During the time that he was Abbot of Gomang monastery the regent Sangye Gyatso, who was under the wing of the Fifth Dalai Lama, was beheaded by the minister Lhasang. It was said that if Lama Jamyang Shadpa had arrived in the Tod-lung area a little earlier than he did, he would have been able to prevent Sangye Gyatso from being beheaded. But some people asserted that because the minister Lhasang was Lama Jamyang Shadpa's patron, the Lama deliberately made his way slowly to the Tod-lung area and thus was too late to intercede in the fateful event.

A similar thing happened during the time of Gyalwang Cho Je Thinlay Gyatso of Sera Med, the spiritual master of Sharchen Ngawang Tsultrim to whom he gave teachings when requested. When Gyalwang Cho Je was indicted by Desi, Sharchen Ngawang Tsultrim didn't lift a finger to help his spiritual master. Desi was actually Sharchen Ngawang Tsultrim's patron. If the latter had intervened in the case, Gyalwang Cho Je probably wouldn't have been in such trouble, but he did nothing.

The great lamas of those times probably had their own political agenda. They may have seen a good reason at the time to behave as they did, and the fault can be seen to lie with the patrons. The conflicts which arose among them usually can be attributed to the fact that the lamas paid consideration above all else to their patrons. Even now, many people spread false rumours about the two immaculate lamas, Rating Rinpoche and Tadag Rinpoche, who are both my lamas, for no good purpose. Such rumour-mongering causes the propagators to take a lower rebirth.

People become embroiled in conflicts while attempting to please their patrons and seeking to fulfil some aim or to attain privileges and rank. Dharma activities like hearing, contemplating and meditating degenerate in the process, giving rise to anxiety and discontent in the practitioners themselves and the community around them. This is a direct result of the disadvantages of the practitioner being linked with several families and one or more patrons and developing a close relationship with these people. That is why we are advised in the Bodhicharyavatara ('Guide to the Bodhisattva's Way of Life') to "Remain like ordinary people."

> Those whom you have known well for some time must
> be acknowledged when you meet them. After that, remain
> neutral towards them.

This may seem rude, but there's a good chance that we will end up in trouble if we chase after our patron like a dog chases the 'Glud'.[14]

There is factional in-fighting on the political stage today also, based on people's personal likes and dislikes. When responsibility is laid at the door of the different traditional schools of Dharma and they are blamed for this and that, it is no different from the events of the past and is really reprehensible. Such conflicts are stirred up by those with a political bent and are not Dharma conflicts per se; but the situation is worsened when people contend that Dharma practitioners are involved in the activities of the political groups.

THIRTY FOUR

Using harsh words disturbs the minds of others and
 causes the character of
Bodhisattvas to degenerate. Therefore, it is the
Practice of Bodhisattvas to abandon abuse
Directed at others which is unpleasant to hear.

We must be very careful not to indulge in harsh, rude or
unpleasant speech because it is unwholesome to do so.

THIRTY FIVE

Habitual afflictions are hard to reverse with an antidote.
So it is the practice of Bodhisattvas to destroy afflictions,
Such as attachment and others, as soon as they appear,
By bearing the antidotal sword of mindfulness and
 introspection.

This stanza uses a metaphor to explain how negativities can
increase through our familiarity with them and how they then
become hazardous and difficult to overcome through the use of
antidotes. We must blow out a fire when it is small; or, as the old
saying goes, we must dam the water while it is still merely a small
stream. The metaphor compares the person to mindfulness and the
antidotes to weapons that the person can use to destroy negativities,
such as attachment and so forth, as soon as they arise.

This process of attacking negativities such as attachment in their
early stages is also discussed in the Commentary on Geshe Langri
Thangpa's 'The Eight Verses on the Training of the Mind':

In all actions, may I search into my mind and, as soon as
afflictions or mental distortions arise, thus endangering
myself and others, may I face them at once and avert
them.

From here onwards the text is summed up in this way:

THIRTY SIX

In brief, wherever one is and whatever one's behaviour,
One should always possess mindfulness and introspection
To examine the condition of one's own mind. In that way,
It is the practice of Bodhisattvas to achieve benefit for
others.

Our mind is accessible to us and so we should assess its state wherever we are and at all times. We should investigate to see whether an inappropriate thought has arisen, particularly a thought which harbours ill-intent, or whether we are being hypocritical—saying one thing and thinking another—and also whether our physical actions are wholesome or not.

If we detect some negativity, we should remind ourselves that, "I have some slight faith and devotion to the Mahayana teachings and have been born in the Land of Snows where there is union of the Mahayana sutra and tantric Dharma; I rely upon many spiritual masters, have received oral transmissions and am adorned with the instructions and textual explanations given by great Indian scholars. If despite this I behave badly, I will undoubtedly be deceiving all the wonderful Bodhisattvas."

We should take on the burden of responsibility ourselves in this way. Try to maintain mindfulness and be conscientious in this effort always.

In the Bodhicharyavatara ('Guide to the Bodhisattva's Way of Life') it says:

O you who wish to guard your minds,
I beseech you with folded hands:
Always exert yourselves to guard
Mindfulness and alertness!

We should exert ourselves in being mindful and, upholding this mindfulness, accomplish as much as possible in the way of working for others. In short, we should sacrifice our body, possessions and all wholesome deeds for others' sake, and offer all the potential of our three doors to sentient creatures, without looking for or reflecting on anything other than what is explained here. After that, we should make a dedication.

THIRTY SEVEN

It is the practice of Bodhisattvas to dedicate the virtue
Achieved by endeavouring in this way to Enlightenment,
In order to eliminate the sufferings of limitless migratory
beings,
With the wisdom of the purity of the three spheres.

We should take all the wholesome activities which we have
accomplished through our sincere efforts to follow the Thirty Seven
Practices of a Bodhisattva, and rather than dedicating these wholesome
deeds to our own long life and freedom from sickness, we should
dedicate them to the endless and infinite numbers of migratory
beings who have fallen into suffering. In this way we dedicate our
positive merit to help others eliminate all suffering and its cause,
knowing by our wisdom the non-inherent existence of the dedicator,
the act of dedication and the recipient of the dedication. From this
viewpoint, it is said, we should go ahead and make the dedication.

This has covered the actual text. Now we bring things to a
conclusion:

I have arranged the Thirty Seven Bodhisattva Practices
for those
Who wish to practise the Bodhisattva path, through
Adhering to the speech of the sublime beings concerning
The meanings related in the sutras, tantras and commen-
taries.

This text is said to be related to the source of sutra and tantra. The
author says that he has portrayed here the meaning explained in the
sutras, tantra and treatises, following the instructions given by our
pious predecessors in the ways of the Thirty Seven Practices of the
Bodhisattvas. These are to be practised in day-to-day life by those
who intend to train in the Bodhisattva path.

Because I have low intelligence and little learning, this is
Not a poetical composition that will please the scholars.
However, as I have relied on the sutras and speech of the
Sublime beings, I think this text explains it incontrovertibly.

103

Here it explains that this text has an original source. He says that his lack of innate knowledge and his comparatively small amount of study makes him deficient in rhetoric, fine words or poetic expressions to please the scholars. Nevertheless, he has described here the view of sutra and tantra emanating from the speech of the most holy beings, and so he believes this to be the incontrovertible practice of the Bodhisattvas. It seems that he says this here in order to be modest.

> Yet, because it is difficult for someone like me, of low
> Intelligence, to fathom the depths of the great Bodhisattva
>   practices,
> I request the sublime beings to forgive me for the
> Accumulated faults, such as contradictions and
>   unrelatedness.

As he says, if there are any contradictory passages where there seems no connection between the earlier and later statements, or if there is some unnecessary explanation, he requests scholars to be tolerant of this collection of flaws. He asks them to have patience and forsakes his own pride in this way. Next he dedicates his wholesome deeds.

> Due to the virtue arising from this, may all sentient
>   beings,
> By means of the supreme and conventional minds of
>   Enlightenment,
> Become as the Protector Avalokiteshvara who does not
>   abide in the
> Extremes of cyclic existence and solitary salvation.

Ngulchu Gyalsas Thogmed thus dedicated whatever wholesome merit he earned by the composition of this text to all sentient beings, and wished they may generate the mind of relative and absolute bodhicitta. He wished that this may be generated in them afresh if not already present and that it may be increased further if already generated. By virtue of such generation, absolute bodhicitta brings to an end the extremes of cyclic existence, while relative bodhicitta precludes the extreme of salvation for oneself alone. By neither resting in cyclic existence nor salvation for ourself, we attain the great parinirvana or

104

highest state of enlightenment, such as that enjoyed by the spiritual master Avalokiteshvara. This is his mental supplication and dedication.

This text was composed in the sacred cave of Ngulchu by the upholder of logic and the texts, the bhikshu Asanga, for the benefit of self and others. The supplication given by the sponsor of the printing of this work reads as follows:

"The aspiring and engaging mind of bodhicitta is the basis and the core path of Mahayana. By the power of the virtuous action of printing this material out of the genuine wish to benefit others, may the teachings of the omniscient Buddha be spread. This supreme teaching of the union of method and wisdom which contains textual explanations and spiritual realisations is expounded by the immaculate Tsong Khapa. May those dwelling in any part of the world and upholding, preserving and promoting this teaching see all their wishes spontaneously granted, and may they continue to live until the end of existence.

"Moreover, may the temporal and ultimate wishes of the magnanimous Dorje Tsewang, his family and all sentient beings be fulfilled, and may they travel swiftly without obstacles to the land of the three bodies of Buddha."

By making symbolic offerings of mind, body and speech, the patron Dorje Tsewang has requested others to make the dedication to the sponsors of the printing of this text. Therefore, the kind-hearted emanation of Dewa Rinpoche, Lhatsun Tulku, composed this dedication prayer out of gratitude.

Conclusion

I have been giving here a brief explanation of the Thirty Seven Practices of a Bodhisattva. Today I have been talking for the benefit of those who do not know the Dharma. I hope everybody has understood and gained some certainty in the Dharma and that there's no need to repeat it over and over again.

The most important message here is to have a kind heart, since the essence of the Thirty Seven Practices of a Bodhisattva is:

> What is the use of our own happiness when all mothers who have been
> Kind to us since beginningless time are suffering?

This is the main point, actually. We should learn to consider others as more important than ourself and act in as kindly a manner as we can, being humble and warm-hearted.

Practising Dharma is the way to have a productive life; we practise in order to be a good person from lifetime to lifetime. Those people who are courteous, kindly and self-effacing and have the sincere intention to benefit others are really practising the Dharma. On the other hand, it is unproductive to say that we are genuinely seeking the Dharma while actually going here and there like a tourist. The reason behind seeking out the teachings of Dharma is to practise them and that practice should merge with the actual Dharma. Do you understand? You should bear this in mind.

You will have understood some of what I have said over the past few days and some of it you won't. Nonetheless, you should try to understand as much as possible by remembering and reflecting on it. If you show the benefit of these discourses by practising extensively what has been explained here from now on until you die, and in however many lives you have yet to live, then my purpose in giving these discourses has been fulfilled.

I know of one man who attended the Kalacakra initiation in Bodh Gaya last year who has really changed since then: his temper has decreased; he has given up alcohol and gambling; he has stopped

106

telling lies; he has become less avaricious and more self-effacing. All in all, he has stopped leading a wasteful life and has become a very good man. It's good to discuss an example such as his with others, whereas it is of no benefit to talk about someone who went to Bodh Gaya and experienced no improvement in his life. We must be careful about this.

It is my duty to talk to you all and I have talked as much as I can here. I have tried to speak in a manner which is productive and easy to follow, because it is important to give teachings that relate to people's day-to-day way of living. There is little benefit in giving Dharma talks which are irrelevant to our lives. So I have adopted a style which uses simple, colloquial language, and sometimes I have even used bad and taboo words. It is my nature to be frank in thought and speech, and I'm always saying that I don't have a seal on my mouth. But I am talking openly here with the express purpose of helping your practice, making improvements in your minds as well as your lifestyle. That is why I put some effort into my techniques of teaching, and then I feel that I have done my duty to the best of my ability. I ask your forgiveness if I have used some harsh, coarse or rude words in my teaching. I have made some mistakes and my words on occasion may have been unreasonable. There is nothing I can do about that except apologise, as it is said: "I mean no disrespect to you, so please have patience with me if something has hurt you."

We are not forcing the Dharma on anyone through this teaching. A disciple attending to the teachings "should have an intelligent and honest mind, and an interest (in the teachings)." This is stated in the `Four Hundred Stanzas'. Whoever listens to the Dharma should be truthful and have a discerning mind able to discriminate between right and wrong, and an active interest in the subject. Obviously you all take a genuine interest in Dharma, because you have endured hardships to come here; whether or not you also have a discerning mind varies with the individual.

Even though no one in this audience of Buddhists and non-Buddhists holds a complex or impenetrable philosophy, nevertheless there may be people who are from the Nyingma school and identify themselves exclusively as Nyingmapas, so that they are reluctant to take an interest in the teachings given by a Gelugpa. Conversely, on occasions where a Nyingmapa gives a discourse, Gelugpas who attend the teachings may dislike him for that reason. They don't feel like paying heed to him because of the Nyingmapa influence, even though his eloquent speech actually benefits their minds. Such an attitude is the sign of a non-discerning mind.

Of course, people often choose to follow one tradition as far as their practice is concerned, and that's a different matter. But I don't hold with people being stubbornly attached to their own traditional lineage in terms of attitude. Some people came here expecting the discourses to be on the Graduated Path, and I'm sure it's highly likely that they would have been disappointed when they learned that the teachings were to be on the Thirty Seven Practices of a Bodhisattva instead.

This is a particular example, showing that we do have a tendency to be partial in our minds, rather than completely entering into the Dharma. Thinking divisively, 'We are this,' and 'They are that,' among Dharma practitioners is really poisonous, an extremely negative attitude. It causes so many people to be reborn in the lower realms, and so it is vital to have an astute, discerning mind. Do you understand?

Those who act with an unprejudiced mind possess one quality of the perfect disciple. It is also important to have discriminating awareness with regard to speech, so that we know what is right and what is wrong speech.

That which is known as Buddhadharma is founded on reasoning, so that when we give Buddhist teachings we are not engaged in coercing others. The Lord Buddha himself said: "Like a goldsmith, who analyses his gold by cutting, rubbing and burning it, so do bhikshus and wise ones analyse the teachings thoroughly, without accepting them out of respect for the teacher."

So, today, you should not automatically respect my words just because they are spoken by His Holiness the Dalai Lama. You should investigate to see whether the teachings given here sound reasonable to you or not and whether they will benefit you when put into practice. If they do seem reasonable, then take notice of them. If they don't, pay no heed to them.

The Lord Buddha himself made a definitive statement on this subject: "Explore the words I have spoken here through investigation.

108

If you find they suit your mind and are beneficial, practise accordingly. If they do not benefit you, then let them be." I am saying the same thing to you now.

Fundamentally, you need to feel the benefit of these teachings. If you do, then the words I have spoken have been worth saying. If you have derived no benefit from them, they are useless; for the purpose of the Dharma is to pacify one's disturbing thoughts and to balance the mind.

I have said so many things over the past three days which should help you to tame your mind and to discriminate between good and bad, so that you abandon the bad and adopt the good things. Choosing between kindness and unkindness, you should try to act always with a kind heart and forsake cold-heartedness. These two things are important. Do you understand?

Notes

1. Body, speech and mind.

2. 'cho gos' is the yellow upper robe worn by all monks and nuns, also known as 'la gos'. 'nam char' is the yellow upper robe worn only by fully-ordained monks. 'thang gos' is the name given to the lower robe worn by monks and nuns.

3. These attitudes are like that of: a wise son; vajra-like; the ground as foundation; a stable mountain; a servant; a staircase; a watchdog; a broom; a good friend.

4. Freedom from the two obscurations—see Footnote No 6.

5. The five certainties are the five definite features of a Sambhogakaya Buddha, namely: 1. Of place: these beings always reside in the richly-adorned Buddhafield known as 'heaven below none'; 2. Of body: they are always adorned with the 32 major and 80 minor marks; 3. Of time: they live for as long as samsara continues to contain sentient beings; 4. Of teachings: they always teach the Dharma of the Greater Vehicle; and 5. Of disciples: they invariably teach a circle of Arya-Bodhisattva disciples.

6. The first obscuration comprises the delusions hindering us from gaining liberation, such as attachment, anger and ignorance; and the second comprises our habitual negative tendencies, which prevent us from attaining the omniscient state. These two obscurations are purified in the final three pure bhumis on the path to Buddhahood.

7. The uncontaminated virtuous qualities of the Arya beings.

8. The period of existence when beings lived for 80,000 years.

9. The power of regret; the power of reliance upon the Triple Gem; the power of the opponent force (to afflictions, such as circumambulation, prostrations and the recitation of mantras); and the power of promise, or commitment.

10. The worlds of beings existing under, on and above the earth.

11. Nirvana or the state of liberation brings inner freedom, but the enlightened individual continues to function in relation to external phenomena, both sentient beings and objects.

12. The six drawbacks are: the suffering of uncertainty, of dissatisfaction, of repeatedly dying, of repeatedly being born, of repeatedly experiencing highs and lows, and of lacking company. When condensed into three they are: the suffering of suffering, the suffering of change, and pervasive suffering.

110

13. The master Nagarjuna and his disciple Aryadeva, founders of the Madhyamika philosophy; Asanga, who founded the Chittamatrin school, and his brother Vasubhandu who composed the text of the Abhidharma Kosha; Dignaga, Vasubhandu's disciple and founder of the school of Buddhist logic (as distinct from the Indian system of logic), who composed the Nyaya pravesh nama pramana prakranama and Pramana samucchaya; Dharmakirti, composer of the principal debating text, the Pramana vartika, which is still studied in today's monasteries; and Yonten Wod and Shakya Wod, who were upholders of discipline.

14. A ritual including a replica of a human being made out of dough (which dogs chase after as food) and offered as a substitute to demons and spirits in order to rid oneself of obstacles.